Morality and Ethics in
Early Christianity

Sources of Early Christian Thought

A series of new English translations of patristic texts essential to an understanding of Christian theology

WILLIAM G. RUSCH, EDITOR

The Christological Controversy
Richard A. Norris, Jr., translator/editor

The Trinitarian Controversy
William G. Rusch, translator/editor

Theological Anthropology
J. Patout Burns, S.J., translator/editor

The Early Church and the State
Agnes Cunningham, SSCM, translator/editor

Biblical Interpretation in the Early Church
Karlfried Froehlich, translator/editor

Early Christian Spirituality
Charles Kannengiesser, editor

Understandings of the Church
E. Glenn Hinson, translator/editor

Morality and Ethics in Early Christianity
Jan Womer, translator/editor

Morality and Ethics in Early Christianity

Translated and Edited by
JAN L. WOMER

FORTRESS PRESS
PHILADELPHIA

Library of Congress Cataloging-in-Publication Data

Morality and ethics in early Christianity.

(Sources of early Christian thought)
Bibliography: p.
1. Christian ethics—History—Early church, ca. 30–600. 2. Christian ethics—History—Early church, ca. 30–600—Sources. I. Womer, Jan L., 1939– . II. Series.
BJ1212.M67   1986   241ʼ.0411   86–45903
ISBN 0–8006–1417–8

2668686   Printed in the United States of America   1-1417

Contents

Series Foreword

Christianity has always been attentive to historical fact. Its motivation and focus have been, and continue to be, the span of life of one historical individual, Jesus of Nazareth, seen to be a unique historical act of God's self-communication. The New Testament declares that this Jesus placed himself within the context of the history of the people of Israel, ushering into history a new chapter. The first followers of this Jesus and their succeeding generations saw themselves as part of this new history. Far more than a collection of teachings or a timeless philosophy, Christianity has been a movement in, and of, history, acknowledging its historical condition and not attempting to escape it.

Responsible scholarship now recognizes that Christianity has always been a more complex phenomenon than some have realized, with a variety of worship services, theological languages, and structures of organization. Christianity assumed its variegated forms on the anvil of history. There is a real sense in which history is one of the shapers of Christianity. The view that development has occurred within Christianity during its history has virtually universal acceptance. But not all historical events had an equal influence on the development of Christianity. The historical experience of the first several centuries of Christianity shaped subsequent Christianity in an extremely crucial manner. It was in this initial phase that the critical features of the Christian faith were set: a vocabulary was created, options of belief and practice were accepted or rejected. Christianity's understanding of its God and of the person of Christ, its worship life, its communal structure, its understanding of the human condition all were largely resolved in this early period known as the time of the church fathers or the patristic church (A.D. 100–700). Because this is the case, both those individuals who bring a faith commitment to Christianity and those interested in it as a major religious and historical phenomenon must have a special regard for what happened to the Christian faith in these pivotal centuries.

The purpose of this series is to allow an English-reading public to gain firsthand insights into these significant times for Christianity by making available in a modern, readable English the fundamental sources which chronicle how Christianity and its theology attained their normative character. Whenever possible, entire patristic writings or selections are presented. The varying points of view within the early church are given their opportunity to be heard. An introduction by the translator and editor of each volume describes the context of the documents for the reader.

It is hoped that these several volumes will enable their readers to gain not only a better understanding of the early church but also an appreciation of how Christianity of the twentieth century still reflects the events, thoughts, and social conditions of this earlier history.

It has been pointed out repeatedly that the problem of doctrinal development within the church is basic to ecumenical discussion today. If this view is accepted, along with its corollary that historical study is needed, then an indispensable element of true ecumenical responsibility has to be a more extensive knowledge of patristic literature and thought. It is with that urgent concern, as well as a regard for a knowledge of the history of Christianity, that Sources of Early Christian Thought is published.

WILLIAM G. RUSCH

I.

Introduction

As the Christian community began to take shape and to expand in the first century, it confronted cultures that already had well-defined religious beliefs, ethical principles, and legal systems. Indeed, this confrontation continued in the ensuing centuries and may be seen clearly in our own day, especially in Western countries, where a multiplicity of cultures and religions are found in most urban areas.

In this volume we have a few of the many documents from the early centuries of Christianity that deal with a variety of themes related to morality and ethics. Christians, in their struggle to develop their self-identity, had to confront the religious and ethical teachings of Judaism, classical Greek philosophy, and a host of Greco-Roman religious cults. How are Christians different? In what ways, if any, are they similar? From its inception, Christianity was more than a new philosophical system or a reinterpretation of Judaism. It was a religious movement that demanded that each adherent's life reflect faith in Jesus of Nazareth as the Messiah. The earliest Christians lived with this personal faith and trust in Jesus, their risen Lord, and his message of the good news. In addition, they saw themselves as being called into a community of believers with whom they lived and shared their faith and their actions. Their faith and life were permeated with the eschatological belief that God's power was at work in their lives and in all the events of history. The Christian community, the church, was being led by God to the fulfillment of his divine purpose. Moral law came from God and was an integral part of creation itself. Unlike much of Greek philosophy, Christianity looked upon ethics as part of the relationship to God rather than as an independent discipline. As we see in the documents, these beliefs provide a foundation upon which early ethical thought and moral rules were built.

From the documents we also see the attempts of various writers to compare Christian morality with that taught by other religions and the classical philosophers. Even in the time of Theodoret of Cyrrhus (d. ca. A.D. 466) we see a bishop's tirade against ancient lawgivers and his favorite foe, Plato.

Side by side with the definition of Christian ethics there is also the development of the underlying theology that supported the need for a moral life and that explains the rewards and benefits such a life offers. This relationship between belief and practice is an important aspect of the development of Christian doctrine as well as of the history of Christian ethics. The two cannot be separated, for they developed hand in hand. Why are the alms given by a Christian different from those given by a pagan? It was not enough to point out that Jesus commanded his followers to love their enemies, to give food and shelter to those in need, and to sell all their possessions and give to the poor. Such actions not only were a sign of loyalty but also would bring eternal salvation, for they were the fulfilling of the Lord's command. The theology behind such actions then developed further. They came to be seen as the way one could eradicate the stain of minor sins. Hence the action leads into the wider theology of sin, grace, and forgiveness, the division of sins into major and minor, and the development of penitential discipline within the church.

As the Christian community grew, it also had to develop an organizational and administrative system. Here we see the emergence of a professional ministry that came to include deacons, presbyters, and bishops. In turn, there were councils that attempted to bring consensus and unity among the clergy and congregations in various geographic areas. In the Council of Elvira we see a series of canons that attempted to define the Christian life and morality for Christians in Spain about A.D. 306. Not only must the morality of the laity be regulated but there is also the need to instruct the clergy regarding their personal lives. Bishop Ambrose of Milan was quite willing to face this challenge in his work, *The Duties*. The growth of the monastic movement during the fourth century also presented theological and ethical problems for the church. Primarily a lay movement, monasticism divided Christians into two major categories: those leading the higher life of perfection and those who remained ordinary laity living in the secular world. Saint Basil's *Letter 22: On the Perfection of the Monastic Life* gives us a glimpse of the morality expected of those who had chosen the life of renunciation.

In the continuing encounter between Christians and secular society, other, more specific ethical issues emerged. We see in Clement of Alexandria an attempt to reconcile what had become rather standard Christian interpretation of Scripture related to wealth with a growing sociological phenomenon. The majority of Christians came from fairly humble backgrounds during the earliest centuries. It was easy for them to look upon the more affluent with disdain and to point out how correct Jesus was when he said it would be difficult for a rich person to enter the kingdom of God. When the wealthy began to be attracted to Christianity in larger numbers, it was necessary to decide whether or not they should first sell all they possessed and give to the poor. Was this action a prerequisite for baptism? Would it become a prerequisite for gaining eternal life? Or could the theology of poverty be developed into a theology of affluence with an emphasis upon the right use of possessions and wealth?

In Augustine's *Letters to Boniface* we see a part of the dissension that arises when one considers war and the military. Can a Christian be a soldier? Can a soldier become a Christian and remain in the military?

The struggle of the early church is the continuing struggle of the church today. What is distinctive about Christian morality and ethics? We see in the documents before us a wide variety of attempts to answer this question. For each of them it is a challenge to show that Christians act out of faith, and it is this faith in God and in Jesus Christ that makes Christian morality distinctive.

The terms "morals" and "ethics" are frequently used interchangeably. In the documents before us we often find instructions related to specific actions, for example, murder, adultery, or stealing. I refer to such dos and don'ts as morals and moral behavior. Behind such admonitions we discover a more reflective and often nebulous array of interpretations that attempt to provide an overall understanding of the reasons for the moral actions. Why should Christians obey a certain moral law? What correlation exists between faith and a Christian's everyday actions? This overview of the Christian faith and life becomes "ethics." It is quite clear in many early documents that their main concern is to provide simple lists of moral commands. It becomes more complicated when we attempt to unravel the ethical and theological implications surrounding the particular commands or instructions that a given writer chooses to emphasize.

A final word should be included regarding the translations. In an attempt to present the documents with a flow similar to modern language, I have, at times, used a very free paraphrase. This has helped avoid the tedious repetition of phrases and the often interminable string of indirect or prepositional phrases. The biblical quotations are translated from the document itself and at times will bear little resemblance to modern English translations. Some words present special problems because of a long tradition regarding their translation. They usually involve topics that are also charged with emotion, for example, homosexuality, abortion, and fornication. Παιδοφθορέω, normally translated as "sodomy" or "homosexuality," I have translated literally as to "corrupt boys" or "sexually abuse boys." Πορνεύω, usually rendered as "fornication," has been translated as "sexual immorality." Words or phrases usually translated as "abortion" are translated literally.

THE NEW TESTAMENT BACKGROUND

As Peter preached on the Day of Pentecost, his witness to the power of God, manifested in the resurrection of Jesus of Nazareth, brought his listeners to the point where they questioned their own faith and commitment. "What should we do?" was their response. "Repent, be baptized in the name of Jesus the Christ and each of you will receive forgiveness of your sins and the gift of God's power in the Holy Spirit" (Acts 2:37–39). The lives of the early Christians revolved around such faith: they trusted that Jesus was the Lord who brought them new life and forgiveness; they believed that God would guide their lives through the power of the Holy Spirit as they participated in the life of the Christian community.

The believer's faith was built upon several assumptions. There

4

was the belief that God had sent Jesus into the world as a gift of divine love and righteousness. It was to this loving and righteous Lord that the individual responded both with intellectual assent and with a moral life. There was little differentiation between faith and life or between belief and morals. Often the ethical understanding of the Christian was not much different from that of Judaism. The themes of love and justice were found in both traditions, and the admonitions of the Mosaic law relating to the widow, the orphan, and the indigent were likewise accepted by Christians as being of great importance. In addition, the place of almsgiving in the life of the faithful was stressed in both Judaism and Christianity. The Christian, however, had a distinctive view of God and of God's love for the whole world, manifested in the sending of the Son (John 3:16). The follower of Christ responded to this divine love with a variety of feelings. There was the desire to be obedient to the commands of the Lord; there was the promise of reward and eternal life to those who remain faithful; there was the response based upon love, human love returned to him who died on a cross and who now lives. The law of the Old Testament was not abolished but was used selectively and expanded in the Christian interpretation to focus upon love of God, love of neighbor, and the leading of a life built upon love (1 Corinthians 13). The Christian lived in a new age: the kingdom of God. Those who were part of this kingdom would receive eternal life, and those who did not enter it would be condemned. The individual was called into the kingdom by the good news and needed only to answer the invitation to "repent and believe." By accepting baptism one was then united with Christ in the new life.

Can you understand that when we were baptized into Jesus Christ we also shared in his death? We were buried with him in death in order that we might rise to a new life just as he was raised from the grave by the glory of the Father (Rom. 6:3–4). Belief in the presence and the power of the Holy Spirit in the believer's life became a vital aspect of New Testament ethics. Anyone who possessed this Divine Presence in his or her life would obviously reflect this in various ways. Paul attempted to summarize such "fruits of the Spirit" in traits like love, peace, joy, patience, kindness, goodness, fidelity, gentleness, and self-control (Gal. 5:22). The Spirit's action, however, was not looked upon solely as a gift to the individual but was also considered a gift to the whole community. The God-given gifts and talents that certain individuals possessed were to be used for the building up of the whole church. For the early Jewish Christians it was only natural that such an emphasis on community should remain an integral part of their religious life. "You are a chosen race, a royal priesthood, a holy people, and a people whom God has chosen" (1 Peter 2:9). As we shall see, this understanding of community remained an important part of Christian theology and ethical teaching, especially during those centuries when Christianity struggled against persecution and government antagonism.

The ethical understanding of the New Testament writers does not present a well-developed or consistent pattern. We can detect a variety of approaches to Christian behavior and morality. Some were inclined to turn the teachings of Jesus into a new legalism; others saw the gospel as a way of being freed from the law and an opportunity to exercise individualism. Another theme continuing throughout the Christian tradition was the imitation of Christ. Saint Paul appealed to the Corinthians, "Follow my example, as I imitate Christ's example" (1 Cor. 11:1). Jesus' love, humility, patience, and obedience were prime examples of the Christian life.

One important theme for later Christian understanding is not found in the New Testament or during the early centuries. This is the concept of transforming society and the world. We shall see that such thought could emerge only as historical circumstances altered the pressures on Christian self-understanding. During the first three centuries, prevailing Christian thought looked upon the world as an alien place. Christians continued their daily life and work within society, but they stood apart from it, "chosen out of it" and often suspicious and hostile toward it (John 15:18–19). The Christians' basic concerns were salvation, eternal life, faithfulness to God and their Lord, self-discipline, and the welfare of the total Christian community, the church. The belief that Christ would soon return was of more concern than the transformation of secular society.

The earliest Christians realized that they were small in number, mainly of the lower class, and almost completely lacking in economic or political power. It was only after this situation began to change that the Christian church developed a drastically different view of its relationship to, and role in, secular society and politics.

THE SECOND CENTURY

As the Christian community entered the second century, the themes we saw in the New Testament period were continued, and new circumstances led to further development in the interrelated areas of theology, ethics, and church organization. The numbers of believers had grown, and there was expansion into Asia Minor, Greece, Macedonia, and on to Rome.

In those writings commonly ascribed to the Apostolic Fathers, we see the strong conviction that the writers were following the teachings of Jesus the Messiah; and from these instructions they received both guidance and edification. These teachings were seen as the basis for ethical understanding and a discipline to be followed in living a moral life:

> Jesus said, "Be merciful, so that you may obtain mercy; forgive, so that you may be forgiven. Whatever you do, others will also do to you. As you give, so shall you receive; as you judge, so shall you be judged; as you show kindness, so shall kindness be shown to you. . . ." From these commandments let us take strength to walk humbly in obedience to His words. . . . (Clement of Rome *Epistle to the Corinthians* 13)

One's manner of life could lead either to condemnation or to eternal rewards:

> Be careful, my friends, so that his many gifts do not lead to our condemnation because we have not done what is good and well pleasing to him with lives full of concord and worthy of him. (Clement of Rome *Epistle to the Corinthians* 21)

> How blessed and wonderful are God's gifts! Life in immortality, splendor in righteousness, truth with boldness, faith with confidence, purity with holiness . . . What are the things prepared for those who wait for him? The Creator and Father of all ages . . . knows their number and beauty. Let us therefore strive to be numbered among those who wait for him, so that we may receive a share in the gifts he has promised. (Clement of Rome *Epistle to the Corinthians* 35)

Ignatius of Antioch (martyred ca. A.D. 110–17) stressed the relationship of action to one's faith in Jesus Christ and saw Christian morality built around the concepts of faith and love:

> What I write is not unknown to those who have perfect faith in Jesus Christ and his love, the start and finish of life. The beginning of life is faith and its ending is love, and in God the two are joined into one unity from which all excellence proceeds. No one who professes faith commits sin and no one who has love will hate. "The tree is known by its fruits," and those who know Christ will be known by their actions. It is not what one promises in words but what one does in faith to the end of one's life. (Ignatius *Epistle to the Ephesians* 14)

Even as Ignatius faced martyrdom, his faith found its focal point in the death and resurrection of his Lord, for in the act of martyrdom the Christian most perfectly imitated Christ by loving, suffering, and dying:

> It is better for me to die in Christ Jesus than to become king over all the earth. I seek the Lord who died for us. I desire him who was raised from the dead for our sake. . . . Do not wish me to remain in this world, for I belong to God. . . . Allow me to imitate the suffering of my God. (Ignatius *Epistle to the Romans* 6)

In Ignatius's writings we also see a developing church order based upon the monarchial bishop who represents Christ himself and around whom the Christian community is gathered:

> Where the bishop is present, let the people be gathered, just as the Catholic church gathers around Jesus Christ. You cannot baptize or hold the agape meal without the bishop's being present. What the bishop approves is also pleasing to God so that what we do together is secure and valid. (Ignatius *Epistle to the Smyrnaeans* 7)

The individual was united not only with Christ in his or her life but also with the whole body of Christ. In this dual allegiance the Christian had ethical beliefs growing out of personal faith and commitment, but also the morality expected by the church. The individual was to follow the leadership of the bishop and to work for unity in all matters. Ignatius looked upon this as another means of imitating Christ:

Follow your bishop's leadership; preserve your body as the temple of God; love unity and avoid conflict; imitate Jesus Christ as he followed his Father. (Ignatius *Epistle to the Philadelphians* 7)

Christian morality was seen as a way of life expected of the whole church. As time went on, the authority of bishops and councils was to take precedence over the individual in defining Christian ethics and morals. The church became the instrument by which moral behavior was defined, legislated, and judged.

Forgiveness and Penance

Because ethics and morals were seen as an integral part of the Christian faith, the church struggled, from New Testament times on, with the problem of disciplining those whose behavior or beliefs departed from the norm of the Christian community. The Sacraments of Baptism and Holy Communion provided the focal points from which the early church developed its disciplinary system. Baptism was the action by which the individual not only received forgiveness and the new life in Christ but also was received into the new community:

> The tower you see being built is the church. . . . Listen to why this tower is being built on the water. It is because you have been rescued and will be saved by the water [of baptism], for the tower is built upon the almighty and glorious name. . . . (*Shepherd of Hermas* vision III, iii)

Christians had no problem with the belief that baptism eradicated the individual's past sins. But what happens to one who has made this profession of faith and then reverts to sin? The New Testament had provided a variety of answers ranging from confession to one another (James 5:16); reproof (1 Tim. 5:20); expulsion from fellowship (Matthew 18; Titus 3:10). The seriousness of a sin could be treated as minor or major (1 John 5:13–21) or even unforgivable (Mark 3:29). In Hebrews 6, 10, and 12 there was a rather harsh line taken against those who relapse into sin after they have accepted the faith.

From the early documents we see that minor sins did not present much of a problem, since they were widespread and liable to befall any Christian. One confessed them directly to God and asked forgiveness. Then the role of good works, and especially almsgiving, came to play an important part:

> Almsgiving is good and so is repentance for sin; fasting is better than prayer, but the giving of alms is better than either of them.... "Love covers up many sins, but prayer that comes from a good conscience delivers from death." (Clement of Rome *Second Epistle to the Corinthians* 6)

For many Christians it was inconceivable that a person who had come to faith in Jesus and who had been born again in baptism would ever commit a major sin again (1 John 3:9; 5:18). A rigid condemnation and exclusion of those commiting major sins after baptism continued to be practiced among rigorist groups, such as the Montanists and, later, the Donatists. The mainstream of Christianity soon came to modify any such harsh approach:

> I said to the shepherd: I have heard from my teachers that there is no chance of a second repentance after we receive the first forgiveness of former sins by our entry into the water. He replied: You have heard correctly. That is true. One who has received forgiveness should live purely and not sin again. Since you have asked about such things, I will tell you something more, but it must not be taken as an excuse by those who are going to believe or by those who are already believers. . . . If someone is tempted by the devil and sins even after God's great and holy calling, there is one chance to repent. If that person then continues to sin, there is no chance to repent again. (*Shepherd of Hermas* Commandment IV, iii)

> We must repent while we are alive. We are like clay in the potter's hand. If the clay misshapes or breaks in his hands, he can reshape it. If, however, it has already been placed in the kiln and then breaks, he cannot mend it again. Therefore, while we are alive, let us repent with our whole heart of the evil we have done in this life, so that we may be saved by our Lord while time remains for us to repent. After death we cannot confess or repent! (Clement of Rome *Second Epistle to the Corinthians* 8)

The Shepherd of Hermas seems to indicate a widespread practice of rejecting any second chance for repentance once a person has been baptized. This work, along with the *Second Epistle* of Clement, makes allowance for human frailty and permits one repentance following baptism.

Some converts to Christianity circumvented the rigorist rule by simply remaining catechumens until death approached. At that point they requested baptism with the belief that they would die before temptation led them into sin and loss of the grace they had received. The emerging opportunity to perform one act of penance following baptism provided some hope for those who harbored such fear. This practice of allowing a second penance became the norm until it was replaced by the discipline of repeated private confessions, acts of penance, and absolution.

The actions condemned by the Council of Jerusalem (Acts 15) came to be interpreted as major sins, which could not be forgiven if committed after baptism. These were understood to be idolatry, sexual immorality, and murder. Tertullian, who had once approved of a second penance, moved into the rigorist Montanist group and then attacked those who permitted a second penance to adulterers. He referred to the Shepherd of Hermas as the Shepherd of Adulterers and concluded that anyone who allowed the pardoning of adultery would also have to pardon idolatry and murder. But the mainstream of Christianity came to accept sexual immorality as a forgivable sin.

Cyprian (d. A.D. 258) initially held that those who had fallen into apostasy could not be forgiven by the church but could be forgiven only by God. The Decian persecution had broken out in the autumn of A.D. 249, and many Christians had lapsed from their faith. Cyprian appealed for "peace and tranquillity" before deciding on the question of their reconciliation and penance (*Letter 55: To Bishop Antonianus*). When the persecution ended, many Christians were admitted back into the church after very minor acts of penance, with the belief that the merits of those martyred were sufficient to allow all to be reconciled. "We do not reject the influence that merits of martyrs and the just will have upon the day of judgment when Christ's flock stands before him" (Cyprian *The Lapsed* 17). Cyprian continued, however, by commanding acts of penance from the lapsed sinner. In A.D. 251–52 two councils were held to discuss the problem, and it was agreed that lapsed Christians could be forgiven and reconciled after rather strict and lengthy acts of satisfaction. The second of the "unforgivable" sins, idolatry, now was tolerated in a new way.

The Council of Ancyra (A.D. 314) seems to have removed the last of the three unforgivable sins, murder. The council decreed that someone guilty of murder could be listed as a penitent, receiving Holy Communion as death approached. The church was finding itself to be less a home for the pure and more a haven for those who were sinners seeking forgiveness from God and their sisters and brothers.

Just as the earlier refusal of forgiveness for any major postbaptismal sin had led to the practice of deathbed baptism, so the developing system of a second penance was to fail. Many now began to withold their request for confession and penance until they approached the end of their life. Frequently the rules applying to such postbaptismal repentance allowed for final absolution, reconciliation, and communion at the time of death even if the prescribed period of penance had not been fulfilled.

Increasingly, the church came to be seen as possessing the authority to bind and to loose (Matthew 16; 18; John 20:19–23). By the second century an embryonic penitential system had developed within the Christian community, and although it varied from one area to another, such discipline was the responsibility of the bishops rather than the presbyters. The penitent was expected to make some form of public confession to the whole congregation, but we do not know in what detail this was done. After this confession the person was listed among the group of penitents and refused Holy Communion until the prescribed time of works of satisfaction had been completed. The individual was then welcomed back into the community and received Holy Communion once again.

It is against this background of developing theology and polity that we must view the ethical understandings of the documents from the second century.

The Didache

The *Didache* gives us one of our earliest glimpses of Christian morality and church practice in the post–New Testament period. Scholars do not agree on a date for this work, and proposals range from A.D. 60 to 150. General agreement tends toward a date between A.D. 100 and 150.

There is the probability, however, that this work reflects practices that had already been commonplace for several decades prior to its composition. The writing is a manual of church instruction that opens with six chapters devoted to the "two ways" open to a Christian: the way of life and the way of death. In this section of the work we have one of the earliest Christian treatises on morality. It follows a pattern to be copied in later centuries—the juxtaposition of virtues against a list of sins. This technique appears to have come from a common practice in Hellenistic synagogues for the instruction of proselytes.

One senses the author's pastoral concern for the recent converts and the catechumens. Such new Christians needed to understand that their life was now different from that of the nonbeliever (I. 2–3). They were expected to pay attention to their role in the whole Christian community (IV. 1–5); and they were to exercise a common-sense approach in applying various admonitions to their own lives, doing "what you are able" (VI. 2–3). The life of the individual, as well as the common life of the whole community, was lived with expectation that one must "be ready, for you do not know the hour when the Lord shall return" (XVI. 1).

The *Didache* does not attempt to explain why a Christian should follow the way of life. It is simply a matter of gaining either eternal life or eternal death. The relationship between the Christian and God was not defined or described; it was merely accepted as a fact of the new faith. The various admonitions of the *Didache* reiterate familiar themes found in both the Old and New Testaments. They became a standard moral code throughout the early centuries of Christianity.

The Apologists

When the Christian movement spread from Palestine into the Greco-Roman world, issues arose that demanded a new ethical understanding and practical solutions for everyday moral questions.

We see the first of these problems in the questions concerning Jewish law and the reception of gentile converts into the church (Acts 15). Jewish Christians, accustomed to a tradition that avoided associating with pagans and cultic practices, found separation increasingly difficult as Christianity spread into cultures permeated with religious groups, practices, and ethics. Time and again Christians were warned not to be "led away from the path of life by those who do not know God" (*Didache* VI. 1). When Christians could no longer live in isolation from their neighbors, the church was forced to formulate ethical teachings that would provide guidance to individuals as they chose occupations, socialized with non-Christian friends, rose to positions of affluence and influence, and regulated their daily affairs, including sexual activities. As we read the documents written over the first five centuries, we see that a variety of solutions were proposed either to help Christians as they lived within secular society or to help them withdraw from it. The goal in either case was to maintain the true faith and its morality.

It was not long before the spreading Christianity faced a problem that was to remain crucial until the emperors Licinius and Constantine promulgated the Edict of Milan in A.D. 313 recognizing the legal status of Christianity and granting religious toleration on an equal basis with other religious groups. There was almost continuous conflict between Christians and the state, manifested in a history of encounter and collaboration and an opposing history of confrontation and resistance (see Agnes Cunningham, *The Early Church and the State*, in Sources of Early Christian Thought).

Polycarp's admonition, written before A.D. 155, presented the ideal: "Pray for the emperors, rulers, princes and 'those who persecute you and hate you' and for 'enemies of the cross' so that 'your fruit will be seen by all and you may be made perfect' in him" (Polycarp *Epistle to the Philippians* XII. 3). Theophilus of Antioch expressed it more succinctly: "[Instead of honoring your gods] I prefer to honor the emperor, not by worshiping him but by praying for him" (*To Autolycus* I, XI).

In the course of the second century the church numbered within its membership a group of writers who were well educated in classical learning and philosophy and also in the methods of political rhetoric and maneuvering. These Apologists rose to defend the Christian community as it encountered secular society and the political system and rulers. Their works were in response to a variety of accusations, often based upon false assumptions, which were made against the Christian community.

The Apologists reflect the change to an outward view as it took place within the Christian community. They were now addressing a new segment of society, namely, those with political power and influence who could be approached with an intellectual, reasoned defense of the Christian faith. Their defense was based upon Greek philosophy and secular learning, but its effect appears to have been minimal. There is little evidence that political leaders of the educated classes were greatly moved or influenced by their writings. They tended to stress the moral superiority of Christianity over other religions at the same time that they attempted to prove that Christians were no threat to the state or to established society but rather a positive stabilizing influence.

One of the oldest sources of tension was between Orthodox Judaism and Christianity. The former, represented in the pharisaical legal tradition, claimed to be the "chosen people of God"; the latter, believing that Jesus' teachings superseded the old law, also claimed to be the "chosen people," having been elected anew in Jesus, who called all people, Jew and Gentile, to follow him in faith. Justin Martyr's *Dialogue with the Jew Trypho*, written about A.D. 160, attempts to demonstrate that Christianity fulfills the Old Testament prophecies, especially those related to God's reaching out to all people.

Another task of the Apologists was to relate Christian beliefs and practices to Greco-Roman culture. Using ideas drawn from Platonism and Stoicism, the Apologists attempted to show that Christianity was the true culmination of earlier philosophy and historical development. There had only been glimpses of divine truth until the Divine Reason in Jesus the Logos was scattered among humanity as though it were small seeds. The Greek philosophers had discovered some of these seeds in their reasoning, but they also had borrowed a great deal directly from the writings of the Old Testament.

In terms of ethical understanding, Christians surpassed all others because they followed God's will and not the human drives of envy and desire. "With us there is not the desire for fame, nor do we respond to a variety of human opinions. . . . But you operate from envy and a great deal of stupidity" (Tatian the Assyrian *Address to the Greeks* xxxii). By listing the immoralities and shallowness of pagan myths, the Apologists sought to show the higher logic and truth that were manifested in Christianity and the strict discipline that was followed by its adherents. The satirist, Lucian of Samosata (ca. A.D. 115–200), in a work ridiculing Christians, raised some of the elements of the Christian life which those outside the faith could not understand:

These gullible people believe that they are immortal and will go on living. Therefore, they do not fear dying, and many of them are willing to give themselves up to the authorities. In addition, their first leader persuaded them that they become brothers and sisters when they give up their Greek gods and worship him. . . . They have no concern for possessions and treat them as common property. . . . Any imposter could easily join them and become wealthy by capitalizing on their naiveté. (Lucian *On the Death of Peregrinus* 13)

Aristides of Athens

The *Apology* of Aristides is the earliest known apology in the series of such writings ascribed to the Apologists. Aristides was a philosopher in Athens who composed his *Apology* to present to the emperor. Scholars disagree as to whether this was Hadrian or Antoninus Pius, since both names appear in the manuscripts. The date of the work appears to be between A.D. 125 and Antoninus's death in A.D. 161.

Aristides begins his *Apology* with an account of his meditation upon the works of nature. From this rather Stoic approach he moves to an account of the divine guiding force behind all of creation. He then divides humanity into "races" and attempts to prove that Christians have surpassed the barbarians, Greeks, Egyptians, and Jews in their understanding of God and the relation of the Divine to creation (chap. 2). The barbarians are dismissed because they worship the things created rather than their creator (chaps. 3–7). The Greeks are seen as even worse than the barbarians because their gods are fictional and are often depicted in stories reflecting their weaknesses and immoral behavior (chaps. 8–11, 13). The Egyptians are described as the "most stupid people on earth," since their gods take animal form, and of course, everyone knows that animals do not possess a soul (chap. 12)! Aristides is somewhat more objective in his treatment of Judaism than are the other Apologists. He admits that Jews come closest to the truth in their acceptance of one God and in their imitation of God through works of charity and compassion. But their lives are bound up in observances of the law. As a result, they are led to the worship of angels and not to the true worship of God (chap. 14). Here we have a theme found in the other Apologists as well. Angels are seen as God's agents who care for human beings and for the affairs of creation and life. The concern of the Torah with such matters as society and the regulation of everyday affairs is, therefore, an emphasis on the realm of the angels rather than on those things with which God is directly involved (Justin Martyr *Apology* 2.5). Aristides then makes his point: "The Christians, O King, in their travels and searching, have found the truth . . ." (chap. 15).

We see in Aristides a style of presenting ethical instruction which is quite different from the straightforward lists of vices and virtues of the *Didache*. Whereas the latter work addressed those committed to the faith, Aristides attempts to show the motivation behind Christian ethics and moral rules. In rather simple terms he attempts to offer the why behind the Christian's behavior. Certainly, the hope of eternal life remains a prime motivating force. The recognition of God's goodness and of the reflection of the Divine within creation itself is also of crucial importance. "Since they recognize the goodness of God to them, they are able to see the beauty that is in the world" (chap. 16). There is no god comparable to the God of the Christians, and they await the rewards that will come from their God in the life to come.

Gnosticism

In the mid–second century the church faced threats to its interpretation of morality and the faith both from within and from without. As we have seen, the threats from without came from political and social forces. The Montanist movement, on the other hand, began within the Christian community itself and eventually attracted Tertullian, who became its most eminent disciple. There was also a growing force that came from both within and without: Gnosticism.

Saint Paul had already been confronted with concepts commonly ascribed to the rather complex religious systems referred to as gnostic (γνῶσις, "knowledge"). In Corinth there were those who professed to have superior knowledge that made them more perfect than others. Some of the Colossians believed that angelic powers, deriving from the universe and heavenly bodies, exerted an influence over human lives that even the Christian faith could not override. Another common mark of gnostic teaching was a radical dualism between the world of the spirit and the world of matter. Usually the human body and the world of matter were equated with evil; the spiritual world was seen to epitomize perfection and goodness. In theistic terms there was one god related to creation and the world, the demiurge, and a superior, remote divine being who ruled the spiritual realm.

During a period when Christianity was beginning to come to grips with an ethical understanding of how to live in the world and face the pressures that the world presented to the Christian faith and life, the gnostic teachings were a regression to inward looking, exclusivist attitudes that encouraged withdrawal from the world. The world was evil and was to be rejected as one attempted to move to the higher spiritual realm of knowledge. In contrast to the Apologists, the Gnostics rejected any idea that the Supreme Being could be seen within human history or knowledge. Some gnostic groups, such as the followers of Saturninus, rejected childbearing, marriage, and the eating of meat, since such actions were related to the inferior world. Others, like Marcion, rejected the Mosaic law and its moral teachings.

From the late first century to the middle years of the second century a variety of gnostic groups developed within the Christian community. Some gnostic leaders, like Marcion and Valentinus, were very capable, and their influence was a major threat to the teachings and practice of orthodox Christianity.

Marcion looked upon the God of the Old Testament as one superseded by the God of love and mercy revealed in Jesus. The Old Testament God was a harsh judge who often reflected inconsistency and a lack of omniscience. It was this God who sent evil into the world through Adam and Eve and who was the author of pain and all sexual activity. Marcion and his followers led ascetic lives, rejecting marriage and sexual relations. In addition, based upon his disdain for the God of the Old Testament, Marcion devised his own list of canonical Scriptures and rejected the Old Testament and parts of the New, mainly those passages that attempted to show a relationship between Jesus' teachings and the Old Testament. He also rejected allegorical interpretation that attempted to give a Christian meaning to Old Testament passages. He believed that the early Jewish Christians had misinterpreted Jesus' relationship to the Old Testament as they attempted to prove that he had fulfilled prophecy and was the promised Messiah of the Jewish people.

Another of the very influential gnostic leaders was Valentinus, who lived in Rome from about A.D. 135 to 165. He presented his teachings as being secret knowledge handed down directly from Jesus himself to a few disciples and passed on to a selected few in each generation. Valentinus did not share Marcion's antipathy toward the Old Testament, but rather, reflecting his Platonic background, was willing to interpret it allegorically. He developed his own standards that allowed him to accept some passages as true while he regarded others as mere fabrications, with no value for the Christian.

In his elaborate system Valentinus believed that the God of the Old Testament was the demiurge, the offspring of Sophia (Wisdom), one of thirty aeons which constituted the spiritual world. Another of these aeons, Christ, became joined with a human being named Jesus who offers saving knowledge to "spiritual people," or pneumatics. These are, of course, his followers who will be able to enter the spiritual realm, the pleroma. Ordinary Christians, who maintain their faith and lead moral lives along with performing good works, will progress only to a minor realm that is under the dominion of the demiurge and not the Supreme Being. They remain as children when compared to the higher individuals who have gained true knowledge. Non-Christians, who possess no knowledge, will come to eternal damnation.

The teachings of Valentinus were very influential within the Christian community at Alexandria by the end of the second century. One writer who attempted to offer pastoral guidance to orthodox Christians in the light of these gnostic influences was Clement.

Clement of Alexandria

Clement (ca. A.D. 150–215) was probably born in Athens of pagan parents, and little is known of his life before he arrived in Alexandria and became a student of Pantaenus, the first head of the catechetical school there, whom he succeeded about the year A.D. 200. Clement's scholarship and broad background brought new depth to the writings of the period. He was well acquainted with Old and New Testament, the postapostolic writings, and the intellectual discipline of philosophy, mythology, and literature. In a period when Christians held much suspicion against secular learning, Clement was able to relate such knowledge to the study of theology and ethics. He argued that the "seeds scattered by the

Logos" were to be found within secular learning. His basic approach, influenced by Platonic thought, is evident in the three books that develop his thought: *Exhortation to the Greeks; The Instructor;* and *Miscellanies.*

In his *Exhortation to the Greeks* he develops a concept of the Logos as it is manifested in Jesus the Christ. As a way of responding to the gnostic emphasis on the need for knowledge and understanding, Clement poses the Word in Christ as the way in which individuals are led from paganism and nonbelief to a relationship with God and, thereafter, to eternal salvation.

In the second work, *The Instructor*, he continues his theme by demonstrating that the Logos is the Instructor who, through love rather than fear, guides the Christian who must face daily life in the world:

> We may designate the Word as being the Instructor. The Instructor is concerned with things practical and not theoretical; with enlightening one's soul in matters of moral goodness rather than merely teaching one's mind. (*The Instructor* I.1)

It is of interest that Clement entitles his work Παιδαγωγός, meaning "one who trains children." Here we see his attempt to respond to the gnostic emphasis on the gaining of knowledge and to the Gnostics' claim of superiority over the "children" who dwell in only the realm of the demiurge. Clement dispels their derision by stressing the positive understanding of being "children of God." We become such children in baptism, and we become the perfect people who gain ultimate knowledge and eternal salvation through Christ.

> When we were baptized we immediately came to perfection because we received illumination—the knowledge of God! We are not imperfect, for we know the One who is perfect. . . . Salvation is to follow Christ. (*The Instructor* I.6)

The instructions that follow are concerned with the Christian's moral development. They range from appeals for moderation in eating and drinking to counsels concerning clothing and appearance and even to rules of etiquette to be followed in the home. In book III, chapters 6–7, he deals with the question of wealth and what this term should mean to the Christian. Frugality, coupled with the individual's own attempts at self-help, is to replace luxuries, such as the use of silver and gold furnishings and reliance on servants.

In the *Miscellanies*, Clement treats an array of subjects randomly. He attempts to show that the Christian, following the Logos Instructor, rises above the false knowledge taught by the Gnostics. The Christian will arrive at the highest knowledge that comes through the love of God. Christian ethics spring from this love; there is striving for the good precisely because it is good and not out of motives based on fear of punishment or the expectation of rewards to those who advance in knowledge.

Clement's *Who Is the Rich Man Who Is Saved?* is an expanded sermon based upon the story of the rich man in Mark 10:17–31. Here he attempts to correct what he considers a narrow and rigorist interpretation of the text by orthodox Christians. It is also a rebuttal of gnostic teachings regarding worldly possessions and wealth. The theme of the story, "If you want to become perfect, sell all that you possess," was seen by many as an appeal for strict asceticism and the rejection of worldly wealth, if not of all possessions. Such tendencies were not only a part of gnostic practice but also part of a long puritanical tradition within the mainstream of orthodox Christianity. Clement, however, developed an interpretation consistent with his other writings. The interpretation is not merely an attempt to make the Markan text more palatable to the affluent members of the church in Alexandria. The right use of wealth and possessions is what is required by God. Those who reflect God's love will use their possessions for the good of others while living disciplined and simple lives themselves. They will divorce themselves from desire for and attachments to wealth and possessions. Instead they will concentrate on being more Christlike.

THE THIRD CENTURY

Montanism

While the church reacted against Gnosticism by developing its theology and polity, it also faced a growing threat from the Montanists, who forced it to come to grips with questions regarding the Holy Spirit, charismatic manifestations and prophecy, the role of the individual within the Christian community, and eschatology.

Montanus and his followers Prisca and Maximilla lived in Asia Minor and gathered around them other followers during the latter half of the second century. They claimed to prophesy under the inspiration of the Paraclete and emphasized the evil times that were upon the world and the imminent second coming of Christ. The intense enthusiasm of the group and its leaders, the emphasis on the problems of the age, and the call to rigid ascetic discipline, including possible martyrdom, all presented an appealing alternative to orthodox Christians who were struggling to remain faithful while living within a non-Christian society. By the beginning of the third century this movement had gained considerable strength and had moved into the Latin churches of North Africa and Rome. Although Montanism was slowly overcome by orthodox Christianity, the rigorous morality was to arise again and again in the church's struggle to maintain ethical standards at times when many people saw the world as filled with moral decay. The monastic movement of the fourth century was to raise the issue once again in a dramatic way.

Tertullian

Tertullian (ca. A.D. 160–225) was born of pagan parents in Carthage. He was trained in classical literature, rhetoric, and Stoic philosophy. His conversion, about A.D. 193, brought a rigid rejection of the classical learning and philosophy of his youth, and he became a staunch defender of what he considered to be Christian truth and morality. Rather than attempting to reconcile Christianity with classical learning, he emphasized the division that existed between them.

Given Tertullian's personal beliefs and inclinations, it is understandable that Montanism held much attraction for him. He joined the Montanists later in life and spent his last years criticizing the laxness of orthodox Christians and their clergy.

The considerable writings of Tertullian reflect his theology from both the orthodox and Montanist periods of his life. He was regarded as the father of Latin theology because of the depth of his thought and his ability to project it in language. In a series of controversial writings he used his rhetorical skills and rigidity to devastate his opponents with ridicule, satire, and arguments that surpassed their defense. In his *Apology*, written about A.D. 197, Tertullian appealed to the rulers of the Roman provinces for toleration toward Christians. He attempted to show that Christians were misunderstood and that they were indeed loyal to both the state and the emperor. They were good citizens, willing to die for their faith rather than bring injury to others through retaliation.

In his work *On Idolatry*, written about A.D. 211, we see quite clearly the belief that Christians must maintain a detachment from many secular activities: "The principal sin of the human race, the greatest guilt in the world, the basic reason for the world's judgment, is idolatry." Tertullian then relates such theological understanding to the daily lives of men and women and the situations they encounter in choosing a career and making a living. Teachers, merchants, craftsmen, and soldiers are all precariously close to idolatry and must exercise considerable care to preserve their Christian faith and morality.

Cyprian of Carthage

Thascius Caecilianus Cyprianus (d. A.D. 258) was converted to Christianity about A.D. 246 and was elected bishop of Carthage just two years later. He was born into a wealthy family and had been trained in rhetoric. Upon becoming a Christian he gave much of his wealth to the poor.

Cyprian was the opposite of Tertullian, who had been the preeminent leader of the North African church a generation earlier. Although Cyprian looked upon Tertullian with great respect and read his writings, his personality reflected a moderation and pastoral sensitivity that Tertullian lacked.

The great Decian persecution broke out in the year following Cyprian's election as bishop. This period led to conflict between the church in Carthage and the church in Rome, and between their respective bishops. There was criticism of Cyprian himself for moving from the city during the persecution, and eventually there was an intense theological debate over the method by which Christians who had lapsed during the conflict should be reconciled to the church. The argument concerning the lapsed led to further questions about baptisms performed by heretics and produced the Novatian heresy and its condemnation of all who had compromised their faith. A new persecution under the emperor Valerian stopped the conflict within the Christian community when Cyprian was beheaded on September 14, 258.

Cyprian's pastoral concern is reflected in his various writings.

The treatise *To Donatus* describes the way in which he was led by God from paganism to the Christian faith. In *The Lapsed* he attempted to define a uniform pattern for reconciling those who had compromised their faith during the Decian persecution. He wanted them to return to the faith—but not too easily. They deserved mercy, but they had to perform penance. In the treatise *The Unity of the Church* we have the most important of Cyprian's teachings. He argues, against heretics such as Novatian and Felicissimus, that the church must remain one, built upon Peter and unified by one organization, the episcopate, and by one faith.

After the Decian persecution there was a severe plague that caused much suffering in the region of Carthage. Non-Christians often blamed such devastation on the Christians for incurring the wrath of the traditional gods. In the midst of this situation Cyprian wrote *On Works and Almsgiving* as a theological statement regarding the place of eleemosynary actions in the Christian faith and life, and also as a practical guide and encouragement to all Christians to help those around them. He draws upon the theological concept that minor sins committed after baptism are purged by good works and almsgiving. This entire process is part of the divine scheme, reflecting God's grace and desire that we should receive his mercy by showing mercy ourselves.

This treatise was widely circulated in the Western church during the centuries that followed, and his approach to good works and almsgiving was carried on in sermons and other writings into the Middle Ages.

THE FOURTH CENTURY

The Council of Elvira

By the beginning of the fourth century, Christianity had spread to both Britain and Spain. This expansion to the far limits of the Roman Empire required bishops to work and act regionally as they attempted to define Christian faith and morals for the various cultures and traditions of their areas. The established tradition and authority we find in the cities and areas where Christians had long resided was not readily accepted in the outlying areas.

The Council of Elvira (ca. A.D. 306) illustrates the attempts of Spanish bishops to regularize a code of Christian morality for both clergy and laity in their area. A time of persecution had just passed, so they wanted to offer guidance to those who had fallen into apostasy and who wished to reenter the Christian community. The problem of idols and idol worship continued and were dealt with in several canons. The Roman civil religion and its system of traditional "flamens," state priests who presided at everything from sacrifices to gladiatorial combat and civil ceremonies, required a series of canons to define the flamens' role for the state on one hand, and their relationship to the church on the other. Although the rules tended to be strict and required long periods of penance, the canons also reflected a practicality and desire to offer encouragement and hope to those who wished to be reconciled to the Christian community after falling away or engaging in a serious breach of Christian morality.

The Monastic Movement

As we have already seen, the church during the first three centuries struggled with the tensions between the world, its demands and enticements, and the Christian faith, with its ideals of pure faith and total commitment. Though the mainstream held both sides in balance, others sought a more rigorist position, especially in regard to the Christian life and moral behavior.

From the mid–third century onward there developed in the church that tradition which has come to be called the monastic movement. It began in the East with such people as Saint Anthony, Saint Pachomius, and Saint Paul of Thebes. During the same period, the heretical sect of Manicheism taught a similar life style. It spread rapidly in the East and on to Rome by the early fourth century. The motivation to withdraw from the world for a life of renunciation and rigid discipline is varied. It was partly the recurring puritanical spirit that emphasized purity and perfection; partly dissillusionment with a church that seemed to grow too fast and become too large; partly a reaction between city dwellers and the more conservative, often simple, folk in the countryside; and partly a rejection of the social structures of the period and the power structures within both secular society and the church. Some of the monks had fled to the desert during persecution and decided not to return. Others rejected their worldly possessions and began a solitary life in imitation of the asceticism of John the Baptist, and of Jesus as he spent forty days in the wilderness.

The movement began as a lay response to the faith, but as the solitary form gave way to community life and structures, the clergy also became a part of the monastic communities. Deacons, priests, and bishops often were chosen from monastic communities, and they in turn reflected this piety in their teaching of the faith and Christian morality.

Basil the Great

Basil (ca. A.D. 330–79) was born of a wealthy family in Cappadocia and began his education under his father, a rhetorician. He continued his studies in the rhetorical schools of Caesarea, Constantinople, and Athens. Two of his brothers were also to become bishops, and his sister, Macrina, was remembered for her ascetic life.

Shortly after beginning his own career as a rhetorician, Basil visited hermit monks residing in the wilderness of Egypt and Syria. He decided to sell his possessions and give the money to the poor, and he himself became a hermit. Others soon came to live near him, and an embryonic monastic community developed. Basil's reputation spread, and he was persuaded by the bishop of Caesarea, Eusebius, to become a priest in A.D. 364. In A.D. 370 he succeeded Eusebius as bishop of Caesarea and metropolitan of Cappadocia.

Many of Basil's writings were concerned with the monastic life. In each of these he was careful to weave New Testament quotations and references with the teachings he offered. His *Moralia* presented eighty rules related to Christian morality and encouraged the ascetic way of life as the best way to live these principles. He also wrote two *Monastic Rules* which attempted to bring some organization and regularity to the life of those living in monastic communities.

In *Letter 22: On the Perfection of the Monastic Life*, written to instruct monks in Christian behavior and morality, we see Basil's remarkable ability to use Scripture as a support for his ideas as well as his ability to define morality in terms that applied equally to monastics and to Christians leading secular lives. The fourth century saw the church come to peace with the state, and the influx of new members into the church required great effort on the part of bishops and priests to instruct these new Christians in both theology and ethical behavior.

Ambrose of Milan

Ambrose (A.D. 339–97), a contemporary of Saint Basil, was the Roman governor of Aemilia-Liguria when, in A.D. 373, he was chosen to become the bishop of Milan. He had not yet been baptized, and he underwent a rigorous eight days during which he was baptized and ordained to the various clerical offices; his consecration as bishop was on December 7, 373. He continued his theological studies under his former teacher, Simplicianus, and became noted as a preacher, teacher, and defender of orthodoxy.

Ambrose spent much of his time combating the teachings of Arianism which were infiltrating into the church. He also attempted to teach Catholic doctrine to the barbarians who were continually moving into the area around Milan. His interest in the growing Eastern monasticism was enhanced by his knowledge of Greek, and he was instrumental in introducing monasticism into the Western church. He was concerned that monasticism remain under the guidance of local bishops and that they continue to offer instruction regarding ascetic theology and practice.

About A.D. 391 he wrote *The Duties of the Clergy*, in which he attempted to offer guidance to those he had already ordained. He used as his model the work of Cicero *De Officiis* and developed his thought under two heads: that of what is honorable and beyond the normal call of duty; and that of what is ordinary and expected of everyone. We see in this work an attempt not only to offer practical moral instruction to the clergy but to show the relationship between Christian ethics and earlier philosophy. It marks a step beyond the usual lists of moral dos and don'ts and illustrates reflection on the philosophical and logical structure that underlies ethical understanding and teaching.

THE FIFTH CENTURY

Augustine of Hippo

In the work of Augustine (A.D. 354–430), we see the flowering of theological thought at a point in history when many movements and influences within both society and the church came to fruition. Christianity had found relative peace in its relationship to the state and, because of its new legal status and respectability, had increased in numbers and in influence within secular society. The monastic movement had secured its place in both East and West, and had established a theological and ethical outlook that constantly influenced, and sometimes challenged, the whole church. The heretical movements of earlier centuries either had passed away or were no longer a major threat to the body of orthodox belief. The challenge of such groups as the Pelagians and Arians was now met with theological arguments reflecting a solid Catholic theological tradition and church structure. Pagan writers, Greek philosophers, and classical literature were all viewed with some objectivity by Christians. Some were rejected or ridiculed; some were adopted and used; others were quoted freely. It is within such a milieu that Augustine was able to develop his own theology and understanding of the Christian faith.

In his *Letters to Boniface* 189 and 220 we see his thoughts presented in a very personal and pastoral way. Combining his concern for a friend, his beliefs about the Christian life, and his regard for asceticism, Augustine attempts to offer guidance to Boniface and to answer the question, Can a Christian remain in the military?

Theodoret of Cyrrhus

Theodoret (ca. A.D. 393–466) was born in Antioch and educated in monastic schools. He entered a monastery at Nicerte about A.D. 416 and was chosen Bishop of Cyrrhus in A.D. 423. He was respected for his pastoral work and his involvement in community activities and development. He was a defender of Antiochene Christology, siding with Nestorius in his conflict with Cyril of Alexandria.

Theodoret is regarded as the last of the great theologians of Antioch, but only a few of his many writings survive. He studied classical literature and knew many of the works of Greek philosophy. His *Cure of the Pagan Diseases* is the last of the apologies from the early centuries, and it is one of the finest; its subtitle is *The Truth of the Gospels Proved from Greek Philosophy*. Quoting over one hundred pagan writers, he compares their answers with those of Christianity to a series of philosophical and theological questions. In chapter 9 of this work he compares Christian ethics with the laws of famous lawmakers in various countries. He attempts to show, often with humorous ridicule, the superiority of the Christian gospel to the teachings of the past.

II.

The Didache

THE INSTRUCTION OF THE LORD TO THE GENTILES

I.

There are two paths to follow: one is life and the other is death. There is a profound difference between the two.

The path of life is this: first, you shall love God who created you; second, love your neighbor as yourself. Do not do anything to your neighbor that you would not want done to yourself.

These words mean this: speak well of those who slander you, pray for your enemies, and fast on behalf of those who work against you. What good is it if you love only those who love you? Even the non-Christians do that. If you will love those who hate you, you will have no enemies.

Guard against the lusts of the flesh. If anyone strikes you on the right cheek, turn the other cheek as well and you will exemplify faultlessness. If someone compels you to go one mile, go another one as well. If someone takes your coat, give up your shirt also. If someone tries to rob you, do not resist even if you think you might prevail.

Give help to anyone who asks you, and do not refuse them. God desires that we help others by using the gifts we have received. We are blessed when we give according to God's command, for then we are blameless. Beware when you ask others for gifts. If you are truly in need, you should ask. If you are not in need, your deception will be judged and you will be placed in prison until you have paid back every penny.

It is written, Keep your gifts to yourself until you are sure to whom you are giving them [Sir. 12:1].

II.

The second commandment of the Lord's instruction is this: Do not kill; do not commit adultery; do not corrupt boys, do not practice sexual immorality; do not steal; do not practice witchcraft; do not use sorcery; do not kill an unborn child by abortion, nor kill a newborn child; do not covet your neighbor's possessions.

Do not perjure yourself; do not give false testimony; do not slander; do not be resentful.

Do not be double-minded or double-tongued, because such deceitfulness is a deadly trap.

What you say should not be false and empty but exemplified in your actions.

Do not take advantage of others, swindle, or be pretentious, malicious, or arrogant. Do not plot maliciously against your neighbor.

Do not hate anyone; some you may reprove; for some you may pray; some you will love more than your own life.

III.

My child, avoid all wickedness and anything like it.

Do not be quick-tempered, for such anger leads to murder; do not be fanatical, or quarrelsome, or hot-tempered, because murders result from such traits.

My child, do not be lustful, for passionate desires lead to sexual immorality; do not be foul-mouthed or look with sexual desire, because such actions lead to adultery.

My child, do not follow fortunetellers, for this leads to idolatry; do not be an occultist, an astrologer, or a witch doctor, and do not become involved with such people, for it leads to idolatry.

My child, do not lie, for lying leads to stealing; do not love money or become conceited, for such traits lead to stealing.

My child, do not be a complainer, for this leads to slander; do not be arrogant or evil-minded, for this leads to blasphemy.

Practice humility, for the humble will inherit the earth.

Be patient and merciful, innocent, quiet and honorable, always paying attention to what you have been taught.

Do not become egotistical or let your life be filled with arrogance. Do not associate yourself with those who are snobs, but walk with those who are just and humble.

Accept willingly the circumstances of your life, and see them as useful, since God is present in them.

IV.

My child, day and night remember those who speak the Word of God to you, and honor them as you do the Lord, for when they speak of the Lord's sovereignty, the Lord is present.

You should study the saints each day so that you may find comfort in their words.

Do not create division, but bring peace among those who are divided. Make your judgments with justice, and do not show favor to certain individuals when you render a decision.

Do not be indecisive in making such a judgment.

Do not be the kind of person who reaches out the hand to receive but who withdraws it when it comes to giving.

From your possessions you should give to others as a ransom for your sins.

Do not be hesitant or complain when you give, but remember who the Paymaster is who gives the reward.

Do not turn away those in need, but be willing to share whatever you have. Do not look upon your possessions as your own, for if you share with others in those things that are eternal, how much more should you share what is temporal.

Do not fail to help your son or daughter, and teach your children to revere God even in their childhood.

Do not give orders to your servants in anger, for they trust in the same God as you and they may lose respect for the God of you both; for God comes to us not according to our status but according to the Spirit who prepares us.

Servants, do the work your master requires, and remain modest and respectful, for the master is an image of God himself.

Hate all that is pretentious and everything that does not please the Lord.

Do not forget to obey the commandments of the Lord, but keep what has been passed on to you without adding to or subtracting from it.

In the congregation confess your sins, and do not begin to pray with a guilty conscience. This is the path of life.

V.

The path of death is completely evil and filled with destruction: murders, physical desires, sexual drives, stealing, idolatries, witchcrafts, sorceries, confiscation of property, false testimonies, pretensions, deceitfulness, treachery, arrogance, malice, egotism, greed, obscene speech, jealousy, immodesty, pride, bragging, and lack of reverence for God.

Opposers of the good; opponents of the truth; lovers of lies; those who do not know the meaning of justice, not holding to that which is good nor executing honest judgment, searching not for the good but, rather, for that which is evil, far away from gentleness and patience; lovers of an empty life, seeking rewards, not showing mercy to the poor, not working on behalf of the oppressed, not acknowledging their Creator; murderers of children; destroyers of God's creation, turning away those in need, oppressing the powerless, allied with the rich; biased judges against the poor, completely sinful—may you be spared from these, my children.

VI.

Watch out that you are not led away from the path of life by those who do not know God.

If you are able to carry the whole yoke of the Lord, your life will be complete. If you cannot do this, do what you are able.

Regarding dietary restrictions, follow what you can. You must, however, avoid all food offered to idols, for this is the worship of dead gods.

III.

Aristides of Athens

APOLOGY

The defense of the philosopher Aristides presented to Hadrian the King regarding God the Almighty. To Caesar Titus Hadrianus Antoninus Augustus, venerable and merciful, from Marcianus Aristides, philosopher of Athens.

I.

O King, by God's grace I was born into this world. I have contemplated the heavens and the earth and the seas, I have watched the sun and the precision of all creation, and I have admired this orderliness.

I am led to believe that the world and all in it is guided by another power and that guiding force is God, who is hidden and kept concealed from us. Everyone knows that the power that guides is greater than the thing that is guided. It is impossible for me to search and discover the nature of this guide behind creation, for such knowledge would be incomprehensible to me. To question the ways in which this guiding force governs creation or to attempt to understand this relationship would still not lead one to perfect comprehension.

I am convinced, however, that this guiding force in the world is the God of all, who has created all people. It is evident to me that this is expedient: we should fear God and we should not oppress other people.

I say that God is not born nor created. God's nature is constant, without beginning or ending; immortal, perfect, and incomprehensible. By "perfect" I mean that God is complete, needing nothing, but needed by everything else.

By saying God "has no beginning" I mean that all other things have a beginning and an end. Anything that has an end therefore disappears.

God has no name, for names are given to things that are created. There are no pictures of God, for any such representations must be based on things that have shape. God is not male or female. God is not relegated to the heavens, for he dwells in all things, visible and invisible. God has no rivals, for there is nothing with more strength than God. God does not possess anger and fury, for nothing is strong enough to demand such a reaction.

Mistakes and forgetfulness are not part of God's nature; rather, wisdom and understanding are the attributes of God, in whom exists everything that does exist.

Neither sacrifices, the drinking of toasts, nor any visible offerings are asked by God. God asks nothing from us, but we ask from God.

II.

Now that we have spoken about God, at least as much as we are able to know, let us look at the human race and see which people believe at least part of the truth we have discussed and which people are in error.

O King, you know that there are four groups of people in the world: barbarians, Greeks, Jews, and Christians. The barbarians trace their religion to Kronos and Rhea and various other gods. The Greeks believe that Helena descended from Zeus and she in turn produced Aeolus and Xythus. Others in the family came from Inachus and Phoroneus, and last, from Danaus the Egyptian, Kadmus, and Dionysus. The Jews trace their origin to Abraham, whose son Isaac had a son named Jacob. Jacob's twelve sons then migrated to Syria and to Egypt. They were given the name Hebrews by their lawgiver but now are called Jews. The Christians trace their religion to Jesus Christ, who is named the Son of God Most High. They believe that God came from heaven and assumed human flesh from a Hebrew virgin. The Son of God dwelt within a human woman. This is taught in the gospel that was first preached among them not long ago. If you will read it, you will understand the power that is in it. Jesus, born of the Hebrew tribe, chose twelve disciples in order to accomplish certain tasks. He was crucified by the Jews, died, and was buried.

They say that he rose after three days and ascended to heaven. In humility and modesty the twelve disciples then went to all known parts of the world and taught about his greatness. Because of this, those who follow these teachings are called Christians, and they are well known.

These are, as I said earlier, the four groups of people: barbarians, Greeks, Jews, and Christians.

The wind is servant to God and fire to the angels, but water to the demons and the earth to human beings.

III.

We will begin with the barbarians and then each of the other groups in order to see which of them believe the truth about God and which are in error. . . .

XV.

The Christians, O King, in their travels and searching have found the truth and, as we see in their writings, are nearer to the truth and perfect knowledge than the other people. They know and believe in God as the creator of heaven and earth in whom and from whom all things exist. There is no other god comparable to their God. They have learned God's commandments, and they live by them in the hope of the world to come.

For this reason they do not commit adultery or engage in sexual immorality or give false testimony or withhold someone's deposit or envy another person's possessions. They honor their father and mother, they are helpful to those around them, and as judges they make decisions with justice.

Christians do not worship idols or images of human beings. Anything they do not want others to do to them, they do not do to others. They do not eat foods offered to idols as sacrifices, for they believe such food to be impure. They console the afflicted and become their friend.

O King, Christian wives are as pure as virgins and their daughters are modest. Christian men do not enter into illegal marriages or other promiscuity, because they await the rewards of the life to come. Out of love for their servants and children, if they have any, they encourage them to become Christians, and if they do so, they are called brothers and sisters without distinction.

They do not worship other gods; they are humble and gentle

and do not lie. They love one another, and they do not disregard their widows; orphans are protected from those who would hurt them. They willingly share what they have with those in need. They bring strangers into their homes and welcome them as true brothers and sisters. Brothers and sisters need not share biological parents but, rather, the same Spirit and God.

Christians, as they are able, provide for the burial of their poor when they die; they provide help to those among them who are imprisoned or oppressed because of their faith in Christ, and they try to secure freedom for them if that is possible.

When there is a person in poverty or need among them and Christians do not have resources at hand to help, they will fast for two or three days in order to provide the food needed.

They are diligent in obeying the teachings of their Messiah, and they follow the Lord their God by living honorably and modestly.

Every morning and at all hours they give praise and thanks to God for the gifts they have received; for food and drink they also give thanks to God.

When a faithful person among them dies, they rejoice and give thanks to God as they accompany the body [to the grave], as though the person were merely moving from one place to another. When a child is born to any of their number, they praise God and, if it should die in childhood, they praise God even more because the child has passed through the world without sin.

If they have one of their number die in guilt or in sin, they weep and cry out for one who goes to face punishment.

This, O King, is the content of the Christians' law and the way in which they live.

XVI.

Because they know God, Christians pray for those things that are suitable for the Lord to give and for them to receive. They continue this throughout their lives. Since they recognize the goodness of God to them, they are able to see the beauty that is in the world.

Truly these are the people who came to know the truth through their travels and searching, and we believe that they alone are close to an understanding of the truth.

The good works they do are not made public to impress others but, rather, are done unnoticed so that they may hide their deeds as one who finds a treasure and hides it [Matt. 13:44]. They make a great effort to be just as they prepare to see their Messiah and receive with great glory the promises he made to them.

It is from their writings, O King, that you may learn of their teachings and rules, the beauty of their worship, and their desire for rewards in eternal life according to their works.

It is sufficient that we have presented this brief survey to Your Majesty regarding the life style and truth of the Christians. Truly great and wonderful is their teaching to the person who willingly examines and studies it. Indeed, these are a new people, and the divine is found in them.

Therefore, take their writings and read them. You will discover that what I have written comes not from myself, nor as their propaganda, but from my reading of their writings and my belief in their teachings and in things yet to come. For this reason I must explain the truth to those who desire it and who look for the world to come.

I do not doubt that the world is supported by the intercessions of the Christians. The other people are in error and cause error, floundering before the forces of nature, because they cannot comprehend anything beyond these natural occurrences. They grope in the dark because they will not recognize the truth, and like drunken men, they stagger, crash into one another, and fall down.

XVII.

Up to this point, O King, it is I who have spoken. For the remainder of what needs to be said, as I already stated, we must look at their other writings, which are too difficult to sum up in brief and which must be understood in relation to actions and not as mere words.

The Greeks, O King, follow shameful practices in having sexual activities with males, a mother, a sister, or a daughter. They attempt to turn the ridicule of their filthiness back against the Christians, but the Christians are just and honest as they persevere for the truth.

Even though the Christians recognize the error [of the Greeks], and are persecuted by them, they bear it with tolerance and even have compassion on them because of their lack of understanding. Christians pray for them that they might turn from their error.

When it happens that one of them is converted, he is ashamed to face the Christians because of what he has done in the past. He confesses to God saying, "I did these things in my ignorance." God purifies his heart, and he is forgiven the sins he had committed in ignorance while he blasphemed and ridiculed the true knowledge of the Christians.

Truly, the community of Christians is more blessed than others on earth.

From now on let those who are conceited and who slander the Christians keep silence. Instead, let them speak the truth. It is better that they should worship the true God than a noise that has no meaning.

What Christians speak truly comes from God, and their teaching is the gateway of light.

Let all those who do not know God come before him and receive the words that are incorruptible and eternal.

Let them prepare for the terrible judgment that will come upon the whole human race through Jesus the Messiah.

The apology of Aristides the philosopher here ends.

IV.

Clement of Alexandria

THE RICH MAN'S SALVATION

1. Those who make flattering speeches in order to impress the rich are, it seems to me, showoffs and victims of their own low self-esteem, for they attempt to gain recognition by praising things that are valueless. Such people are also blasphemous and deceitful. They are blasphemous because they do not praise and glorify God, from whom and in whom all things exist, but rather they give this glory due God to men who wallow in filthy and despicable lives. For this reason they will face God's judgment. They are deceitful because they encourage the rich to delude themselves by showering them with false praise, which causes them to focus even more on their wealth and the admiration it arouses. The affluent are already in danger of being corrupted by self-pride without such deceitful influence. As the proverb says, they are adding "fire to fire" or "pride to pride" and arrogance to the pressures that wealth brings. It would be better if wealth were downplayed and even diminished, for it is a dangerous and deadly disease. The one who exalts and exaggerates himself is in danger of losing everything, as the divine Word declares. It seems to me that we do better if we try to help the wealthy to work out their salvation in every possible way rather than to praise and encourage them in what is harmful to them. First, we should pray that God will grant salvation to the rich, for we know that he will gladly answer our prayer. Then, with the Savior's grace to heal their souls, we should teach them and lead them to the truth. Only those who reach the truth and are distinguished by good works will gain the prize of eternal life. Prayer requires a life that is well disciplined and persevering until the last day of life, and

our life of discipline demands a good and committed attitude that seeks always to follow the Lord's commands.

2. The reason that salvation seems more difficult for the rich than for the poor is complicated. Some people, by only casually hearing the words of the Lord about its being easier for a camel to pass through the eye of a needle than for a wealthy person to enter the kingdom of heaven, suddenly take a look at themselves and see that they are not destined for salvation. They give up in despair and become completely a part of this world, with no concern for the world to come and no interest in the teachings of our Teacher and Master and his description of who the rich really are or how God makes possible what seems impossible to humans. On the other hand, others understand this saying rightly and properly, but they fail to see the importance of works that lead to salvation, and therefore they do not amend their lives as is necessary for those who have this hope. In both cases I mean the wealthy who have learned about the Savior's power and his glorious salvation. I am not concerned with those who have not yet come to understand this truth.

3. It is the duty of all who love truth and who are a part of the Christian community not to treat wealthy members of the church with rude contempt or, on the other hand, to bow to them in order to benefit from their friendship and generosity. Use the Word of God to help them overcome their despair, and show them with interpretation of the Lord's teachings that the kingdom of heaven is not an impossible goal for them if they will obey the commandments. After that you should help them to understand that their fears are groundless for the Savior will gladly receive them if they so desire. Teach them what kind of works and attitudes they need in order to reach their hoped goal. It is a goal within their grasp, but it will require effort! If you will allow me an analogy that compares the insignificant and perishable with the great and imperishable, I would see the rich as athletes. One of them sees no hope of winning and therefore does not enter the race; the other hopes to win but is unwilling to train, exercise, and eat properly, and so fails to gain the prize. The person invested with wealth should not feel that he or she is already excluded from the Lord's prizes. Remain faithful and look at the greatness of God's love toward all people! But do not expect to reach the goal without discipline and effort and without training

and perseverance. Let the Word become your trainer and allow Christ to be the referee of the contest; let the food and drink of the Lord's new covenant become your nourishment; let the commandments prescribe your exercises. Your life should be richly decorated with the virtues of love, faith, hope, knowledge of the truth, compassion, gentleness, humility, and seriousness, so that when the last trumpet sounds to signal the end of the race and our departure from this life, you may stand before the judge with a good conscience as the victor. The judge shall admit you as one worthy of entering the heavenly kingdom, where you will receive the victor's crown amid the acclamations of the angels.

4. May the Savior grant me guidance as I continue my teaching from this point so that I will offer advice that is true, appropriate, and helpful for your salvation. I want to discuss the meaning of hope itself and, second, to help you see how you reach such hope. The Lord gives freely to those in need; he gives understanding to those who ask and dispels their ignorance and despair. His words are repeated again and again so that the wealthy may become interpreters for themselves and understand the words fully. There is nothing better than to listen again to what we have heard before from the gospel. Do not let them depress you as they did when you listened with the uncritical and mistaken logic of immature understanding.

As he went on his way, a man came and knelt before him, asking, "Good teacher, what must I do to inherit eternal life?" Jesus said, "Why do you call me good? No one is good except God. You know the commandments: do not commit adultery; do not kill; do not steal; do not give false testimony; honor your father and mother." The man answered, "I have done all of these things since I was young." Jesus looked at him with love and replied, "You lack one thing. If you want to be perfect, sell all that you possess and give it to the poor, and you will have valuable possessions in heaven. Then come and follow me." His countenance fell immediately, and he went away dejected, for he had great possessions. Jesus looked around and then said to his disciples, "How difficult it will be for those who have wealth to enter the kingdom of God!" The disciples were startled at his words. Jesus said to them, "Children, how difficult it is for those who put their trust in riches to enter the kingdom of God! It would be easier for a camel to move through the eye of a needle than for a rich person to enter the kingdom of God." The disciples were greatly dismayed and asked, "Who then can be saved?" He said to them, "With men it is impossible, but not with God." Peter said to him, "We have left everything we had to follow you." Jesus answered, "In truth I say to you, whoever leaves home and parents, brothers and possessions for my sake and the cause of the gospel will receive a hundredfold; in this life, houses and lands, possessions, brothers, sisters, and persecutions; in the time to come, eternal life. The first will be last, and the last first." [Mark 10:17–31]

Jesus does not accuse the man of having failed to fulfill the law. Instead, he loves him and warmly commends him for his faithfulness. However, this is not sufficient for gaining eternal life, since obedience to law alone, without living a fruitful life, cannot bring one to perfection. Who would deny that works of the law are good? The "commandment is holy" [Rom. 7:12] inasmuch as it provides training and initial instruction that is regulated by fear. This will lead to the culmination of legalism and the emergence of the grace of Jesus [Gal. 3:24]. Christ is the fulfillment of the law and in him all who believe are justified [Rom. 10:4]. Those who do the Father's work are not turned into slaves but are made his sons and daughters and heirs. . . .

10. "If you want to be perfect"—by this Jesus implied that he was not yet perfect, for there are no intermediate categories. "If you want" is a divine affirmation of the free will that the rich man possessed. The decision was his, but the gift was God's. God freely gives this gift of salvation to those who ask for it in sincerity. God does not force it upon us, for he hates the use of force, but he provides for those who seek, and he gives to those who ask and to those who knock. If this is your desire, if it is your honest wish and not a bit of self-deception, you may take what is offered. "You lack one thing," the thing that Christ offers, the good that is above the law and that the law cannot give because it does not possess it. This good is only for those who live in Christ. The man who had lived by the law from his youth and was proud of this accomplishment could not accomplish the one task the Savior gave him in order to reach the eternal life that he desired. He went away dejected, realizing he could not fulfill the requirement that separated him from the life he had requested. His interest was not in eternal life, as he had said, but in the desire to gain respect by

merely raising the question. There were many things he could do with his goal, but he lacked strength and dedication to accomplish the work that would give him life. We also see this when the Savior spoke to Martha, who was busy with many things, preoccupied and distracted with entertaining, and annoyed that her sister sat and listened to Jesus rather than helping with the tasks at hand: "You are troubled with many things, but Mary has chosen a better option and it will be of lasting benefit to her" [Luke 10:38–42]. The Lord asked the rich man to give up his many activities and to concentrate on the one that brought the grace of him who offered eternal life.

11. What was it that caused the man to run away and to reject his teacher, his inquiry, his hope, his goal, and his life of obedience? "Sell all that you possess": what does this mean? It does not mean, as some superficially suppose, that he should throw away all that he owns and abandon his property. He is to banish those attitudes toward wealth that permeate his whole life, his desires, interests, and anxiety. These things become the thorns choking the seed of a true life. It is not a great thing or desirable to be without any wealth, unless it is because we are seeking eternal life. If it were, those who possess nothing—the destitute, the beggars seeking food, and the poor living in the streets—would become the blessed and loved of God, even though they did not know God or God's righteousness. They would be granted eternal life on the basis of their extreme poverty and their lack of even the basic necessities of life! The renunciation of wealth and the distribution of possessions to the poor are nothing new. Even before the Savior's coming this was practiced by such men as Anaxagoras, Democritus, and Crates, who wanted leisure time, or time for acquiring knowledge and study of dead wisdom, or fame and notoriety.

Why then is Jesus' command new or divine and life-giving, whereas the actions of people long ago brought no such benefit? If the new creature, the Son of God, offers something new, what is it? His command focuses not on the visible act, as earlier teachings had done, but on something greater, more divine, and perfect. The soul and mind are stripped of desires, and preoccupations are rooted out and discarded. This is a concept unique to the Ghristian and comes from the Savior himself. In former times some people viewed possessions with contempt and rejected or discarded them, but they allowed their inward passions and drives to become even stronger. They became arrogant, pretentious, conceited, and contemptuous of other people, as though they themselves were superhuman. How could the Savior have recommended things that would be harmful and injurious to those whom he had promised eternal life? In addition, it is possible that one who has given away his possessions will then lament over what has been done and spend much time wishing the decision could be reversed. The wealth has been abandoned, but the realization that it is gone and the longing that it might be returned will become the double irritation of insecurity and regret. When someone lacks the basic necessities of life, the human spirit is broken and the desire for higher things is replaced by the constant searching to satisfy day-by-day needs.

13. How much more productive is the opposite situation, when a person possesses all that is necessary and needs to be concerned not with personal survival but with the needs of those less fortunate! How could there be any sharing if no one possessed anything? Would not such an understanding of possessions contradict and be at odds with other excellent teachings of the Lord? "Make friends for yourselves by using your worldly wealth, so that you will be received into an eternal home when it is all gone [Luke 16:9]. "Store up treasure in heaven, where neither moth nor rust will destroy it and where thieves cannot steal it" [Matt. 6:20]. How can we escape the Lord's condemnation to fire and outer darkness for not feeding the hungry, giving drink to the thirsty, clothing the naked, sheltering the homeless, if we ourselves do not possess these things? When the Lord was entertained by Zacchaeus, Levi, and Matthew, who were wealthy tax collectors, he did not order them to give up their possessions. Instead, he commanded that their wealth be used justly and not for their condemnation, and he promised, "Today salvation has come to this house" [Luke 19:9]. Their wealth, Jesus said, was to be shared in order to provide food for the hungry, drink for the thirsty, shelter for the homeless, and clothing for the naked. If we can only do such things if we first possess wealth, how could the Lord demand that we reject such riches? If we did, we would not be able to share, feed, and lend support! This would make no sense at all!

14. Therefore, we must not throw away the riches that benefit

not only ourselves but our neighbors as well. They are possessions because they are possessed, and they are goods because they are good and provided by God to help all people. They are under our control, and we are to use them just as others use materials and instruments of their trade. An instrument, used with skill, produces a work of art, but it is not the instrument's fault if it is used wrongly. Wealth is such an instrument. It can be used rightly to produce justice. If it is used wrongly, it is the fault not of the wealth itself but of the user. Wealth is the tool, not the craftsman. We must not blame something that is neutral, being neither good nor evil in itself, but must assign responsibility to the one who chooses to use such an item either with care or negligence. As humans, we have the ability to decide how we are going to use what has been given to us. Do not regret your possessions, but destroy the passions of your soul that hinder you from using your wealth wisely. Then you may become virtuous and good and use your possessions in the most beneficial ways. The rejection of wealth and selling of one's possessions is to be understood as the rejection and elimination of the soul's passions. . . .

20. The rich man, who had lived according to the law, did not understand the Lord's teaching figuratively. He could not comprehend how one can be both poor and rich, have wealth and not have wealth, use the world and not use the world. He walked away confused and sad. He gave up his desire for a better life because he felt it was beyond his ability to achieve. He saw a difficult task as an impossible one. It is difficult to keep ourselves from becoming enticed by and dependent upon the life style that affluence offers, but it is not impossible. Even when surrounded by affluence we may distance ourselves from its effects and accept salvation. We center our minds on those things taught by God and strive for eternal life by using our possessions properly and with a sense of indifference toward them.

Even the disciples were at first filled with fear and amazement. Why? Because they possessed wealth? They had already given up their only possessions, their nets, hooks, and fishing boats! Why, in fear, do they ask, "Who can be saved?" They had listened well and as good disciples perceived that the Lord had intended a deeper meaning behind the obscure parables. They realized that they had already fulfilled the command to give up one's possessions, but as newly recruited disciples of the Savior, they sensed that they had yet to control and abolish their desires and passions. Because of this, they were extremely concerned for themselves, just as the rich man was for his need of possessions rather than his desire for eternal life. It was right that the disciples' fear should be expressed at this moment when both those having many outward possessions and those having many internal desires were categorized as being rich and denied entry into heaven. Salvation is reserved for those who are pure and without such passions and desires.

21. But the Lord responded, "With men it is impossible, but not with God." Here we see great wisdom, for it is impossible for us to rid ourselves of all desires and passions. If we make this our goal and earnestly desire and pursue it, the power of God will be added to our efforts. God lends support to willing souls but, if we lose our eagerness, the spirit of God is withdrawn. To save individuals against their will would be an act of force, but to rescue those who desire it is grace. The kingdom of heaven does not come to those who are lazy or asleep, but "men of violence take it by force" [Matt. 11:12]. This is the only good kind of force there is, to force God and to take life from God by force. God knows those who persevere, even violently persevere, and willingly gives in to them, for God welcomes such persistence. Blessed Peter, the chosen, pre-eminent, and first of the disciples, to whom the Lord had paid tribute [Matt. 17:27], heard this and responded quickly, "We have left all and followed you." If Peter meant his own property, he was bragging, for as the tradition goes, he had at most four coins to leave. He has forgotten to count the kingdom of heaven as payment for the coins. As I have been saying, it is by ridding oneself of the old desires and concepts that inhabit the mind and soul that we follow the Master. Then we may seek his sinlessness and perfection and stand before him as we would a mirror, inspecting our soul and arranging everything as he would desire. . . .

26. "The first will be last and the last first." This saying, beneficial for its deeper meaning and interpretation, need not concern us at this point, for it applies to all people who have accepted the faith and not merely to the wealthy. We will reserve it until later. I believe that it has been demonstrated conclusively that the Savior does not exclude the rich on account of their wealth and possessions. He has not set up obstacles to keep them from salvation,

provided they submit to God's commandments, valuing their obligations more than worldly objects. They must fix their eyes on the Lord as a sailor watches the helmsman for his signals and commands. What harm has been done by one who builds economic security by careful planning and frugality prior to becoming a Christian? What is to be condemned if God, who gives life, places a child in a powerful family and a home full of wealth and possessions? If one is to be condemned for having been born into a wealthy family through no personal choice, that person would be wronged by God, who would offer a worldly life of comfort but deny eternal life. Why would wealth ever have been found within creation if it only causes death?

If an affluent person can control the power that wealth brings and remain modest and self-controlled, seeking God alone and placing God above all else, that person can follow the commandments as a poor individual, one who is free of and unconquered by the disease and wounds of wealth. If this is not the case, a camel will have a better chance to pass through the eye of a needle than such a rich person will have of entering the kingdom of God [cf. Mark 10:25]. The camel, passing through a straight and narrow way more quickly than the rich man, has another loftier meaning, which is a mystery taught by the Savior and which I discussed in my *Exposition of First Principles and Theology*.

27. I would now like to explain the initial, obvious meaning of the illustration and suggest why it was used. It teaches the affluent that they must not neglect their salvation with the mistaken belief that they are already condemned; it also teaches them that they need not divest themselves of their wealth or treat it as a bitter enemy of life but, rather, must learn how to use it in order to gain life. People do not perish because of wealth, nor do people gain salvation merely because they think they should receive it.

The Savior, however, offers hope for the wealthy and explains how the unexpected may happen and the hoped-for may become a reality. The Teacher, when asked which was the greatest commandment, replied, "You shall love the Lord your God with all your soul and with all your strength" [Mark 12:30–31], and he pointed out that no commandment is greater than this. That is quite understandable, for the commandment deals with the first and the greatest: God our Father, through whom all things have been created and to whom all things that are saved shall return.

We were loved first by him and have our existence from him. It would be blasphemous to consider any other thing greater or more excellent than him. We give him this small tribute out of gratitude for his great blessings because there is nothing else we can offer to a God who is perfect and who needs nothing from us. The very act of loving the Father to the limit of our strength and power brings us immortality. In proportion to our love of God we are drawn more closely into God.

28. The second commandment, in no way less important than the first, is this: "You shall love your neighbor as yourself" [Luke 10:27]. You must love God more than yourself. When it was asked, "Who is my neighbor?" he did not follow Jewish custom and list such people as relatives, other Jews, proselytes, the circumcised, or the followers of the same law but, rather, told the story of a man going from Jerusalem to Jericho who was stabbed, robbed, and left nearly dead on the road. A priest passed by, as did a Levite. But a scorned and outcast Samaritan had pity on the man and, unlike the others, stopped to help. He provided all that the man needed: oil, bandages, a donkey to transport him, and payment to the innkeeper for his care. "Which of these," Jesus asked, "was a neighbor to the injured man?" When the answer was, "The one who showed pity," the Lord answered, "You must go and do the same" [Luke 10:28–37]. Love should burst forth in good works!

29. In both commandments our Lord speaks of love, but he gives an order to our expression of that love: first we are to love God, and after that we are to love our neighbor. Who else can that mean than the Savior himself? Who, more than he, has shown us pity? We who nearly died because of those earthly powers of fear, lust, hatred, desires, dishonesty, and pleasures. Jesus is the only one who can heal these wounds by completely cutting out those passions down to the root. He does not deal with the outward results, the bad fruit of the plant, as the law did, but his ax cuts to the roots of our wickedness. He has poured wine over our wounded souls, his blood which is from David's vine (the Eucharist). He brought to us the oil of pity from the Father and he pours it upon us in great abundance. He has bandaged us for health and salvation, with love, faith, and hope. As a reward, he has provided angels and heavenly rulers and powers to be at our service. They too are freed from the meaninglessness of the world

through the revelation of the glory of the children of God. We must love him as we do God, for God loves Christ Jesus as the one who does his will and keeps his commandments. "Not everyone who says to me, Lord, Lord, shall enter the kingdom of heaven, but only those who do the will of my Father" [Matt. 7:21]. "Why do you call me Lord, and then never do what I tell you?" [Luke 6:46]. "Happy are those who see and hear what the saints and prophets were never able to see and hear" [Matt. 13:16–17]. You will be happy, too, if you do what I say.

30. Those who love Christ are first; those who love and care for those who believe in him are second. Whatever is done for a Christian is accepted by the Lord as though it were done to himself, for the whole Christian community is his own. "Come, you are blessed by my Father, and enter the kingdom that was made ready for you before the world was made. I was hungry and you gave me food and I was thirsty . . ." [Matt. 25:34].

V.

Tertullian

ON IDOLATRY

I.

The principal sin of the human race, the greatest guilt in the world, the basic reason for the world's judgment, is idolatry. Although each sin has its own distinctive character and will be judged individually, it also falls under one general category, which is idolatry. Do not worry about names of specific actions at this moment, but consider every idolater to be a murderer also. But you ask, Who has been slain? To clarify and add further to the indictment, I would answer, Not a stranger or an enemy, but yourself. How? By error. With what weapon? Offense against God. How many blows? As many as are the idolatries. One who denies that an idolater perishes will also deny that an idolater commits murder. An idolater is also guilty of adultery and sexual immorality, for such a person serves false gods and thereby adulterates the truth. Such falseness is idolatry. The idolater is engulfed in sexual immorality, and because he is allied with unclean spirits, how can he help being polluted and corrupted? It is for this reason that the Holy Scriptures equate lewdness with idolatry [Ezek. 23:49]. It is fraud if someone takes away from someone else or refuses to give someone what that person rightfully should possess. In the secular world such actions are harshly condemned. Idolatry is fraud against God, for it gives others what should be reserved for God, and this becomes an insult against the Divine. If fraud, sexual immorality, and adultery cause death, then idolatry also must be regarded as causing murder. Just as these sins are deadly and swallow up salvation, so all of the other sins may be taken in order and dealt with individually to show that they too fall into the general category of idolatry. A further example would be the uncontrolled sexual desires of the world. What better way to show off our idolatry than with the way we dress? There are also lust and drunkenness that are reflected in overindulgence in food and drink at parties and celebrations. This is injustice! What is more unjust than to disregard the Father of justice? This is vanity, for the whole way of life is vain. This is lying, for one lives a lie when one lives this way. Now you can see that all sins are idolatrous and idolatry is found within every sin. In addition to this we must realize that all sins are in opposition to God and anything opposed to God belongs to devils and unclean spirits. These same devils and unclean spirits belong to the idols, and therefore all who ally themselves with such spirits are also guilty of sharing in their idolatrous nature.

II.

Now we must not pursue the various sins that fall into the category of idolatry. Let us look at idolatry itself, a sin so offensive to God, a basis for so much crime, and a virtual mass of tentacles that reach out in all directions to tempt and take hold of the servants of God. We must beware and shun all of the enticements of idolatry, for they often are undetected or disguised. Too often we think of idolatry only in its most evident forms: burning incense to idols, offering sacrifices, observing pagan feasts, or becoming involved in pagan rites or organizations. This is the same as equating adultery with kisses, embraces, or touching of flesh, or limiting murder to causing loss of blood or the actual taking of a life. We know that the Lord includes much more in the definition of such sins. Adultery includes the way in which we look at someone and the thoughts and sexual desires that fill us; murder includes the harsh and hurting words and the angry actions we direct at someone else. We have lost the love we should have for others and, as John says, "Anyone who hates his brother is a murderer" [John 3:15]. If God did not expand the meaning of these sins, we would be no better than the heathen who, under the guidance of the devil and his wisdom and ingenuity, are willing to punish such crimes. How can our "righteousness exceed that of the scribes and Pharisees" [Matt. 5:20], as our Lord has commanded, unless we have understood the vast meaning of what is unrighteousness? And if the foundation stone of unrighteousness is idolatry, we must reject the many ways in which idolatry manifests itself in the world. . . .

VI.

If there had been no law from God prohibiting our making of idols and if no voice from the Holy Spirit had denounced both the makers and the worshipers of idols, we would still conclude from our understanding of the Sacrament of Baptism that such activities were contrary to our faith. How can we renounce the devil and his angels if we make them? How can we separate ourselves from those upon whom we are dependent in our lives? What kind of tensions have we caused between ourselves and those who provide our employment? Can you deny in words what you have done through your actions? Do you destroy with your words the good works of your hands? Do you preach one God and then make many idols? Do you preach the true God and then make false gods? One may say, "Oh, I make them, but I do not worship them." As if the reason for not worshiping idols were different from the reason for not making them! In either case the sin is against God! Indeed, if you provide idols for others, you are worshiping them yourself. You worship them not with the offering of a worthless perfume but with your own soul, and not with the life of an animal but with your own life. To these false gods you offer up your talents, your libation of sweat, and your wisdom. You have become to them even more than their priest, for you are their creator and your diligence has given them their divinity. Do you still deny that you worship what you created? You may, but these idols do not, for they have received from you a fat, precious, and perfect offering—your salvation.

VII.

Oh, that our zealous faith would force us into mourning when a Christian has left an idol-making workshop to come to the church! That person leaves the workshop of the enemy to enter the house of God! Hands that are the mother of idols are raised in praise to God, and hands that are praised by idol worshipers are used to pray to God. Those hands that fashion bodies for demons reach out to receive the body of the Lord. As if this were not enough! It may be less important that these hands receive from others what they then contaminate, but it is more important when those hands pass on to others what they have defiled. Makers of idols are even accepted into the ministry of the church. What a wicked sin! At one point in time the Jews laid violent hands upon Christ, but these hands insult his body everyday. They deserve to be cut off! Remember the saying: "If your hand offend you, cut it off" [Matt. 18:8]. What hands deserve more to be cut off than those which scandalize the body of our Lord?

VIII.

There are also many other crafts that are related to idols in that they furnish the items incidental to idol worship. Such activities are as sinful as the making of the idol. Some workers build and equip the temple; others decorate it and provide the altar and furnishings. Some prepare the gold leaf, or the ornaments, or the stand upon which the idol is placed. This is the more important work, for it creates dignity rather than merely providing standard equipment for a temple.

If artisans plead that they do such work only because they need a livelihood, they should look for other employment that does not involve idols and idol worship. Such work takes them outside the limits of Christian morality. A plasterer can work repairing roofs, coating walls and cisterns, making relief moldings, wreaths, and other decorations. The painter, marble mason, bronze worker, and every kind of carver know of other ways to use their arts. It is much easier to polish a shelf than it is to form a statue! If one can carve a Mars from a lime tree, why not take less time and build a chest instead? There is no art that is not related to another form of art. One form of craftsmanship is not independent of other crafts. There are as many arts as there are desires in a human being. You will probably ask about wages and the cost of labor. There is a difference in the amount of labor involved in the various crafts. The lower pay can be compensated for by producing more. How great is the market for walls with a niche for statues or temples and shrines for idols? Yet look at the opportunity to build houses, courtyards, baths, and expensive residences. The gilding of shoes and slippers is in demand every day but not the gilding of Mercury and Serapis. Crafts will flourish as they

meet the demands of luxury and pride (which are more numerous than superstitions!). Pride will demand dishes and cups more
frequently than does superstition. More crowns are bought
because of human extravagance than for religious ceremonies.

Since we teach that men should avoid crafts that involve idol
making or that relate to idol worship, we must remember that
some items are used by humans and idols alike. With care we must
not knowingly allow things made with our hands for human use
to be used for idols. If we purposely allow such usage and do not
remedy the situation, we are not free from the contamination of
idolatry, for our hands are in the service and honor of devils.

IX.

We observe that there are other vocations that also may be categorized as idolatrous. I should need to go no further than merely
to mention astrologers. One of them has challenged me, however,
and believes that he should continue in this profession. I do not
accuse him of worshiping idols merely because many heavenly
bodies are named after them. Indeed, he admits that the power of
God rules the heavens and that we should not deny God and
think that our lives are controlled by the stars. My basic concern is
that it was angels, condemned by God for rejecting him and for
being lovers of women, who started this strange belief in the first
place. O divine judgment, which firmly engulfs the earth and
which is acknowledged even by those who do not comprehend
it! The astrologers are rejected just as are their angels. Rome and
Italy have expelled them, just as heaven rejects their angels. The
followers and the masters are both excluded. But you say, Magi
and astrologers came from the East. We know that the science of
the Magi is related to astrology. The interpreters of the stars were
the first to announce Christ's birth and the first to bring him gifts.
Does this mean that they made Christ obligated to them? Where
does this lead? Can we go so far as to believe that their science is
really the science of Christ, which studies his stars and not the
stars of Satan, Mars, and others who died long ago? The science of
the Magi was permitted up to the time of Christ's birth in order
that from then on no person's birth would be related to heavenly
manifestations. The Magi offered to the infant Lord their frankincense, gold, and myrrh as the last sacrifices of the world's glory,

for from that time Christ fulfilled such need for all people. There is no doubt that the Magi were warned in a dream not to return by the normal route to their own country but to return by another way. This was commanded so that they would turn from their past practice. It was not done so that Herod would not pursue them, for indeed he did not follow them and he did not know which way they had gone. We too should learn from this what the right religion and the right way are. It was commanded that they should turn to another way.

There is another kind of magic, which involves miracles. This kind was used against Moses, and it continued to offend God right up to the time of the gospel. At that time Simon Magus became a believer, but he attempted to supplement his work as sorcerer by buying the power of the Holy Spirit imparted through the laying on of hands. The disciples reprimanded him and expelled him from the faith [Acts 8:9–24]. Another sorcerer who came with Sergius Paulus and who confronted the same apostles was punished with blindness. I believe that astrologers would still receive the same reward if they met the apostles! When sorcery is punished—and astrology is one form of it—surely the particular type is condemned along with the broad category. After the coming of the gospel there are no Sophists, Chaldeans, shamans, witchdoctors, or sorcerers who are not openly punished. "Where is the wise person? Where is the scribe? Where is the skilled debater of this day? Has God not made foolish the wisdom of the world?" [1 Cor. 1:20]. Astrologer! you know nothing if you do not know that you should become a Christian. If you know that, you should know that you must reject your astrology. Since those beliefs attempt to foretell the crises facing others, they should also foresee their own fate. You have no part nor lot in your system [Acts 8:21]. You cannot hope for the kingdom of heaven if you use your finger or magician's wand to misuse the heavens.

X.

We must also have a look at schoolteachers and professors of learning (*litterarum*), for their work has a close relationship to idolatry—first, because they must teach about the gods of the nations by discussing their names, genealogies, traditions, and attributes. Teachers then observe the rites and festivals of these gods because their income is dependent in part on such activities. What schoolteacher does not take a table of the seven planets and attend the Quinquatria festival? The first tuition payment from a new student is then offered to honor Minerva. The teacher may not be considered a devotee of a certain god but is still an idolater. Is there less defilement in that situation than there is when a business is dedicated publicly to a particular god? The Minervalia is as much Minerva's as the Saturnalia is Saturn's, and the latter festival must be observed by even the lowliest servants. Teachers must also participate in the gifts connected with New Year's, the Feast of the Seven Hills of Rome, the winter solstice, and memorial days. On the feast of Flora the school is decorated with flowers, and the wives of the flamens [civic priests] and magistrates offer sacrifices. The school receives gifts on specially designated days as well as on the birthday of an idol, and thus every pomp of the devil is satisfied. Who will assume that such activities are befitting a Christian except one who believes they are fitting for someone who is not a teacher? We know it may be said, If it is not lawful for servants of God to teach literature, neither should they learn from it. How can one then inquire into human knowledge or learn anything if one does not use literature? How can we abolish the secular studies that are necessary as a part of divine studies? Let us see what parts of a literary education are necessary and which are to be avoided. A believer can learn from literature without teaching it, for the principle of learning is different from that of teaching. If a believer teaches literature, the teaching can easily be interpreted as supporting, affirming, and giving recognition to the gods being discussed. The teacher thus gives recognition to the names of the gods, and the law forbids us to utter their names [Exod. 23:13], for this takes in vain our God's name. Faith in the devil is taught from the earliest education. Ask if one who teaches about idols is not committing adultery! When a believer hears such things, if he or she understands what idolatry is, he or she will reject them. For one who is still learning as a new believer there must first be study about God and the faith. Then these things can be rejected, and the believer will be as safe as guests who know that they are receiving a cup of poison from a host who does not realize its contents, and therefore do not drink it.

Some argue that out of necessity one must study literature in order to learn. It is much easier not to teach than not to learn literature, and it is easier for the believing student to avoid the harmful activities of the school than it is for the teacher to stay away from them.

XI.

Let us look at other sins and the way in which they began and developed. The first is covetousness, the "root of all evils" [1 Tim. 6:10], which overpowers some and shipwrecks their faith. The apostle teaches that covetousness is idolatry [Col. 3:5]. Next is lying, which is the servant of covetousness (I will not deal with false oaths, since it is not lawful to take oaths at all). May the servant of God be involved in making profits? What is the reason for acquiring possessions other than covetousness? When the motive for seeking profit and possessions is taken away, there will be no reason for commerce or trade. There may be some necessary reasons for trade that are free from anxiety over covetousness and lying. But that commerce which revolves around the very soul and spirit of idols and the worship of every demon is idolatry; in fact, is it not the chief of all idolatries? Some items such as frankincense and other foreign materials used in idol worship are also used in medicine and even by Christians in the burial of the dead. Such trade will continue. When you supply materials for the processions, priests, and sacrifices of idols, are your dangers, losses, inconveniences, anxieties, running around, and business itself anything other than the service of idols? Let no one argue that this requires the abolition of all trade! Sins which are the most serious must receive attention commensurate with the danger they pose. Some require that we not only avoid committing them but that we also avoid those things through which they may be committed. Even though something is done by others, it makes no difference, if I made it possible. I should not give support to someone who is doing something I myself should not do. If I am forbidden to do it, I should take care that it is not done through me.

Finally, in another example, which is equally dangerous, I offer the same advice. Since I am forbidden to indulge in sexual immorality, I should not encourage or support others who do. I am resolved not to indulge in illicit sex myself and therefore I cannot be involved in procuring sexual partners for others or in any other profit-making operation related to sexual activity.

Likewise, the prohibition against murder shows me that trainers of gladiators must be kept out of the church, for they are as guilty as the fighters themselves. Here is a more pointed example. Suppose that the person who provides victims for the public games were to come to the faith. May he continue in his trade? Or if a Christian decides to begin such a business, would you allow him to remain in the church? I assume you would not, unless you are also willing to overlook those who sell frankincense. The one provides the blood, and the other the incense. Before idols were constructed, idolatry was epitomized in the selling of incense, and even now it is the burning of incense, rather than the presence of a statue, that perpetuates idolatry. Therefore, does not the seller of incense serve demons, since it is his product that does more to continue idol worship than the provision of idols themselves? We appeal to the conscience of every Christian! How will the believer who sells incense react when he enters a temple? Will he spit and blow at the altar that smokes because of the incense he provided? How will he exorcise his own foster children [i.e., the demons], whom he stores in his own house? If he thinks he throws out a demon, he should not congratulate himself, for he has not destroyed an enemy. Since he provided the food of incense to that demon everyday, it should have obeyed his request! No craft, profession, or trade that supplies materials for the making of idols or their worship can be free from being condemned as idolatrous, unless we attempt to define idolatry as something other than the serving and worship of idols. . . .

XVIII.

Now we must speak about the clothing and insignia related to idolatry. Each person has appropriate clothing for use in daily affairs and for special offices and occasions. The Egyptians and Babylonians wore purple, gold, and ornaments around their necks as signs of their status; and so our own provincial priests wear garments with borders or stripes, and palm-embroidered robes, and golden crowns. But there is a difference. The former were presented by kings as symbols of honor (and so we speak of the purple given by kings, or the "candidates" who wear our own *toga candida*) and were not considered the apparel of priests or of others who served idols. If they had been, those who were holy and faithful would have refused the polluted garments, and it would have been seen much more quickly than it was at first that Daniel did not serve idols or worship Bel and the dragon. The use of purple garments among the barbarians was a sign not of high office but of noble birth. Joseph, who had been a slave, and Daniel, who during his captivity came to be quite important, both came to be free men in Egypt and Babylon and wore the dress of the barbarian nobility. Therefore, if need be, believers may allow boys and girls to wear traditional robes as symbols of birth and not of power, of family and not of status, of position and not of superstition. But the purple and other symbols long associated with the power and honor of idols are profaned. Robes with borders, stripes, and broad bars are even used to dress up the idols, and symbolic banners or staffs are carried before them. This is fitting, for the demons are the rulers of this world and the purple robes and symbols are a part of their equipage. What do you gain if you wear the garments but deny that you perform the tasks associated with them? You cannot appear to be clean when you are covered with the unclean. You may put on a garment that is dirty within itself and not because of you, but it will leave its dirt on you.

Those of you who use Joseph and Daniel as examples to refute me must remember that things old and new, rough and polished, just begun and already completed, for slave and for the free, are not always capable of being compared. Those men of old were forced to be slaves, but you are servants of no one, for you are Christ's alone and he has freed you from the captivity of the world. For this reason you live by his commandments. The Lord walked in humility and without worldly honor or even a place to call his home, for "the Son of man has nowhere to lay his head" [Matt. 8:20]. His clothing was simple, for he said, "Behold, those who wear soft clothing live in king's houses" [Matt. 11:8]. As Isaiah had said, "He was without a pleasant appearance or beauty" [Isa. 53:2]. He did not claim any right to exercise power over his people but became their servant; he knew he was a king but refused to be proclaimed a king; he showed his people how to reject pride and power and the pretense of attire and honor. Who would have had more right to use such honors than the Son of God? What symbolic items, and how many of them, should escort him, what kind of purple should radiate from his shoulders, what gold should glisten on his head if he had permitted and not rejected such glory for himself and for his people! That glory which he did not want for himself, he has rejected; that which he rejected, he condemned; and what he condemned he equated with the pomp of the devil. He only condemned what was not his own, for what does not belong to God belongs to the devil. If you renounced the pomp of the devil (at baptism) remember that any part of that pomp which you touch is idolatry. Let this realization remind you that all the powers and honors of this world are not only alien to God but enemies of God. They are used to punish God's servants, and because of them the wicked shall face unknown punishments. Your birth and your possessions become a problem for you as you resist idolatry. There are many remedies to help you in this struggle, and should they seem weak, there is a greater one. It is the promise of a greater dignity that is given to you not on earth but in heaven.

XIX.

In the previous section we have raised an issue that concerns military service, since it involves both dignity and power. We therefore need to pursue this point more fully. Is it possible for a believer to become a soldier or for a soldier to become a Christian? Is it possible for a low-ranking soldier, who is not obligated to offer sacrifices to idols or carry out capital punishment, to become a Christian? There is no relationship between the Christian's oath and the soldier's oath, the sign of Christ and the sign of the devil, the camp of light and the camp of darkness. One soul cannot be divided between two masters—God and Caesar. If we wish to debate the subject, you may point out that Moses carried a rod, Aaron wore a buckle, John wore a leather belt, and Joshua, the son of Nun, led an army. But how could a Christian soldier go to war or keep the peace without the sword that has been taken away by the Lord? Even though soldiers came to John [the Baptist] and received instructions for their conduct and even though a centurion became a believer, our Lord, when he took away Peter's sword, took away the sword of every soldier. No uniform can be worn by us if it is the dress worn to perform acts that the Lord has condemned.

XX.

Since our conduct is judged not merely by our deeds but also by our words (for it is written, "Behold the man and his deeds," and, "Out of your mouth you shall be justified"), we must remember that even in our words, habit or fear may allow idolatry to enter in. The law forbids the naming of pagan gods. This does not mean that we cannot even say the name, for this would be very difficult in everyday talking. We say, "You will find him in the Temple of Aesculapius," or, "I live in Iris Street," or, "He has been made a priest of Jupiter." Such names are a part of our everyday vocabulary, and people are even given such names themselves. I do not honor Saturnus if I call a man by that name. That same is true of Marcus. What the law says is, "Take heed to all that I have said to you; and make no mention of the names of other gods, nor let such be heard out of your mouth" [Exod. 23:13]. This means that we do not call them gods. In the first part of the law it says, "You shall not use the name of the Lord your God in vain [Exod. 20:7], that is, as the name of an idol. Whoever honors an idol with the name of God has become an idolater. If I must use the names of idols, I must make it clear that I am not recognizing them as gods. Even the Scriptures name various gods but add "their" or "of the nations," as David does when he says, "But the gods of the nations are idols" [Ps. 96:5]. I have pointed this out as a preliminary to remarks I shall make later on.

It is an evil habit to say such things as, "By Hercules," or, "By Jupiter," for some people do not realize that they are offering an oath to Hercules. What will such an oath be, when taken in the name of gods you have rejected, than a mixture of your faith with idolatry? You are in fact showing honor to those whose names you use in making an oath!

APOLOGY

XXXVI.

If some who are called Romans are found to be enemies of Rome, why are we denied the name Roman on the pretext of being considered enemies? The answer cannot be that we are denied the name because we are enemies, since some who have the name are really Rome's enemies.

The loyalty, reverence, and fidelity due to the emperors are manifested not in token actions that even an enemy could perform but, rather, in those actions that God commands us to offer to all people.

Our actions of good will are not merely for emperors. We do not reserve special treatment for certain individuals, since what we do impartially is done for ourselves and the praise or rewards that come from God and not from others.

We treat the emperors as we would any neighbor. We are forbidden to desire harm, to do evil, to speak or to wish malice against any person. The things we would not do against the emperor we may not do against anyone else either. Likewise, what is not to be done against another person would be even worse were it committed against someone God had made to be so great.

XXXVII.

If we, as Christians, are commanded to love our enemies, as I have already stated, who is left that we could hate? If we are forbidden to retaliate against someone who injures us, for fear of sinking to their level, whom can we injure? Think about your own experiences. How often do you react cruelly and violently against Christians partly because of your own emotional response and partly in response to the laws? How often does the hostile mob disregard your advice and go ahead, taking the law into its own hands and inflicting injury against Christians with stones and fires? With the riotous behavior of the Bacchanals, they do not even allow the Christians who are dead to rest in the tomb but remove their decomposing bodies and cut them into pieces and scatter them.

Yet, can you point to any instance when we have retaliated for the injuries we have received even though we remain a united and resolute community who could in a single night return evil for evil by setting fires out of vengeance? As a divinely gathered group we do not even consider resorting to human revenge or avoiding the suffering that tests our faith. If we desired to become open enemies, do you think we would have problems finding support and people willing to fight? The Moors, the Marcomani, the Parthians, or any other single race of people who inhabit a given territory probably easily outnumber us since we are spread all over the world! As a group of people we are newcomers, but we have filled what you considered to be yours—your cities, islands, fortresses, towns, marketplaces, camps, tribes, professions, palaces, senate, and forum. The only thing we have left to you is your temple. What war is there that could defeat us who are eager and ready to do battle even against the odds? We are willing to die for our faith since we are convinced it is better to be slain than to kill someone else. We do not need to arm ourselves and resort to insurrection, for we can merely disagree with you and resist peacefully, and the battle will continue with the tension that is created. If our multitude had broken away from you and moved en masse to a far-off corner of the world, the loss of so many citizens, no matter what sort they were, would have brought shame to the Empire, nay, even inflicted punishment on the Empire by virtue of the mass desertion.

You would be panic-stricken when you realized the silence that fell upon your society and economy and the feeling that your world had died. You would have to find other subjects to rule, and you would have more enemies than citizens. Right now you have few enemies, because a vast number of the inhabitants you have scattered in your cities are Christians. Yet you choose to call them enemies of the human race rather than enemies of human error. Who else could help deliver you from those secret enemies which seek to destroy your minds and ruin your health? By this I mean, who would save you from those spirits of evil which we drive away without seeking payment or reward? If we truly wanted vengeance we would merely allow the unclean spirits to overrun you. Yet you do not consider rewarding us for the protection we offer, nor do you recognize that we are an asset to your society. We pose no threat to you. Instead you look upon us as enemies, failing to realize that we are enemies of human error and not of the human race.

XXXVIII.

Therefore, should not Christianity be treated more gently and be recognized as one of the legal religions, recognizing that Christians do not commit crime or ally themselves with illegal and harmful movements?

Unless I am mistaken, such movements are prohibited as a way of maintaining public order and of protecting the state from disruptive factions. Such groups could disturb elections, councils, the senates, public gatherings, and even the public shows and games, where rival clashes could occur. Especially at this time we see that some people make their living by taking part in demonstrations and violence.

We do not seek fame and honor, nor do we care to take part in your public meetings. Affairs of state are of no interest to us, for we are concerned instead with the whole world that encompasses all humanity.

We avoid your public spectacles because they have developed out of superstition and we do not wish to recognize or celebrate the events behind the spectacles. We do not talk about, watch, or listen to the madness of the circus, the immodesty of the theater, the violence of the arena, or the vanity of the gymnasium.

Why are you offended because we take pleasure in things different from you? Surely it is our loss if we do not seek amusement in the ways you do! You allowed the Epicureans to practice their understanding of true happiness. Does it matter if Christians have pleasures too?

XXXIX.

Now that I have refuted the charge that Christians are evil, I would like to continue and show the positive good that they do. We are a community united by our religious faith, our unity of discipline, and our common hope. We gather together in our congregations to come as a multitude to burst into God's presence with our prayers. God is pleased with such a mob! We pray for the emperors, their ministers, and for all in authority, as well as for the welfare of the whole world, for peace on earth, and for the delay of the end of the world. We meet together to read our Sacred Scriptures and to apply their message to our lives as a reminder of how we should live or a warning as to what the future might bring. In either case our faith is nourished by the words of Scripture, we are given new hope and confidence, and our way of life finds support in the precepts given by God. When we gather, there are not only admonitions but also warnings and God-given condemnations. The judging of wrongdoing is very important to us, as it must be to all who believe that God knows their thoughts and actions; and we go even further at times and banish some sinners from sharing in our prayer, our assembly, and all holy fellowship. Such extreme action is but a foretaste of the future judgment.

Our leaders are elders of proven character who reach that office not by buying support but in recognition of their integrity, for nothing of God's can be bought with money. Even though we have a community treasury, it is not made up of money paid as entrance fees or dues. Each member may bring a monthly donation, if he or she so desires, as a voluntary offering. You might say that these gifts are concrete manifestations of a person's devotion. The funds are never used for banquets or drinking parties or for operating an eating house but, rather, are used to feed the poor and bury them, to help boys and girls who have no parents or property; the funds are used for servants who have grown old and mariners who were shipwrecked. In addition, the fund assists those in mines, on islands, or in prison for the sake of God's love, as a pension coming from their faith. It is because of these works of love that some put a brand upon us. "See," they say, "how they love one another." They are amazed because their lives are filled with hatred. They also say of us, "See how they are ready to die for one another." This they cannot understand, for they are ready to kill one another. They even deride us because we call each other brothers, probably because they use such names to refer to a blood relationship, the only way they can recognize any degree of affection. But we are your brothers as well, since we are all human beings, even though you, because of your evil, are hardly worthy to be considered human. On the opposite side are those brothers who acknowledge one Father of all, one God who unites them in one spirit of holiness and who has brought them out of a common womb of ignorance into a common experience of the awesome light of truth. Perhaps we are considered to be less than true brothers since we cannot shout about a tragedy that molded us as brothers or because we become united in what we possess as a family, whereas you are usually divided from one another because of dissension over deciding the family inheritance. We who are united in heart and soul have no hesitation in sharing

what we have. All things are held in common among us except
our spouses. In this regard we give up our community partner-
ship, whereas other people here practice a form of community by
taking the wives of their friends and by giving their own wives to
their friends. This, I believe, follows the teachings of the wise
men and philosophers of ancient times. Socrates the Greek and
Cato the Roman shared their wives with their friends (I do not
know if the wife consented or not) in order to provide children in
the other household as well as their own. How can one have
regard for chastity when it is given away so freely by another?
What an example of Athenian philosophy and Roman dignity
when a philosopher and a government magistrate became pimps!
It is no wonder that you belittle the love Christians have for one
another. You also condemn the simple meals we share together,
by calling them extravagant and occasions of debauchery. The
saying of Diogenes seems to apply to us: "The Megarians feast as
if they were to die tomorrow, but they build as though they were
never going to die." One sees so much more easily the speck in
another's eye than the log in one's own. The air around us stinks
from the belching of so many tribes and social groups. The Salii
will eat themselves into debt; you need accountants to figure out
the tithes and offerings for Hercules; the Apaturia, Dionysia, and
Attic assemblies need a gourmet cook; the smoke from the Serapis banquets will call out the firemen. And yet it is the modest
dining room of the Christians that attracts your attention! Our
meal is explained in the Greek word that we use for it: love. No
matter what it costs, it is of benefit to religion since it provides
nourishment to those in need, not as it is with you who act like
parasites as you glory in selling your freedom so that you can stuff
yourselves at a banquet where you have to endure the bad manners of those around you. In our meals a special respect is paid to
the lowly, just as it is with God. If the intent of our feast is worthwhile, you need to consider also the other rules that we follow. It
is a religious act, and therefore nothing rich or disorderly can be
allowed. We begin, even before we sit down, by praying to God.
We eat only an amount necessary to satisfy our hunger, and we
drink only what is necessary and modest. Only enough is eaten to
satisfy the appetite, since we remember that the worship of God
is to follow later in the night. The talk at table is as though the
Lord was present. After the water is brought in for washing the

hands and the candles are lit, each person is invited to sing a hymn to God as best he or she can, using either one from Holy Scripture or one of his or her own composing. This proves that we have not been drinking heavily! Just as we began, we also end with prayer. We leave not as a riotous mob ready to assault the innocent, or to roam the streets and create destruction, but with orderliness and modesty, as a people fed on virtue rather than a party of food and drink.

These meetings of Christians deserve to be ruled illegal if they follow the same pattern as the destructive and illegal actions of other groups. But can you point to people who have been harmed by our gatherings? We act the same when we come together as we do in our scattered lives; we are as a congregation just what we are as individuals: we do not harm others nor do we harass them. When the upright, the virtuous, the pious, and the pure gather together, you should not call them a divisive faction in society but should, rather, consider them an assembly of the highest order.

VI.

Cyprian of Carthage

ON WORKS AND ALMSGIVING

1. Many and great are the gifts that have been and still are given to us by God the Father and Christ for our salvation! The Father sent his Son to rescue us and to give us life so that we might be restored to him. The Son was willing to be sent as the Son of man so that he could make us sons of God. He humbled himself so that a devastated race might be raised to life again; he was wounded so that he could heal our wounds; he became a slave in order to free those in bondage; he accepted death so that he could give immortality to mortals. These are the many and great examples of divine compassion! But, in addition to this, his great compassion and love also provide the means by which we are given further support even after we have been redeemed. When the Lord came to earth, he healed the wounds that Adam had given to humanity and he provided an antidote to the poisons of the old serpent. He gave a law to those who had been made whole and commanded that they should sin no more, for fear of worse things that might happen to the sinner. We were limited and confined by the restrictions of our naiveté. Our weak human strength had to be supplemented with the divine mercy that was given once again to guide us toward salvation. We have been given works of justice and mercy to do, so that our almsgiving will wash away the stains we receive in our lives.

2. The Holy Spirit speaks in the divine Scriptures and says, "By almsgiving and faith sins are purged" [cf. Prov. 16:6]. Those are not the sins that we committed earlier, for they were forgiven by Christ's blood and sanctification. It also says, "As water extinguishes a fire, so almsgiving atones for sin" [Sir. 3:30]. Here it also

69

shows us that, just as the supply of saving water quenches the fire of Gehenna, so also the flame of sin is smothered by almsgiving and works of justice. Because in baptism the remission of sins is granted once and for all, so in works of charity that flow from the baptized person, the mercy of God continues to be manifested. The Lord teaches this in the gospel when he responds to a criticism that the disciples eat before washing their hands: "He who made the outside also made the inside; give alms and everything is clean for you" [Luke 11:41]. This has taught us that not the hands but the heart should be washed so that the dirt within is removed, and not merely that which is on the outside. Those who are clean on the inside will be clean on the outside as well. If we cleanse our mind, the cleansing of our skin and body will also begin.

Furthermore, he admonishes us and points out the way in which we may become clean and purified: by the giving of alms. He who teaches and warns us in mercy asks us to show mercy, and he who seeks salvation for those whom he already redeemed at a great price, teaches that they may be washed a second time if they have soiled themselves after receiving the grace of baptism.

3. Let us acknowledge, dear friends, this saving gift of divine mercy. Since none of us can be free of some wounds to our conscience, let us receive the healing that washes away our sins. None of us should flatter ourselves with the belief that we have a pure and spotless heart or that we are innocent and without need of healing for our wounds. It is written, "Who can say that they have a pure heart or that they are free from sin?" [Prov. 20:9]. John says, "If we say that we have no sin, we deceive ourselves, and the truth is not in us" [1 John 1:8]. If no one can be without sin, even those who are proud or foolish and do not admit it, we can see how necessary and compassionate the divine mercy is toward us. God knows that those who were healed in baptism will suffer more wounds in life, and he has provided additional remedies to save them.

4. Beloved friends, the divine instruction of both the Old and New Testaments has never compromised or failed in admonishing God's people to works of mercy. The Holy Spirit calls and exhorts each of us to hope for eternal life and to give alms. God commanded Isaiah, "Cry aloud, do not give up. Lift up your voice like a trumpet and declare to my people their transgres-

sions, and to the house of Jacob their sins" [Isa. 58:1]. God commanded that their sins be condemned and the divine wrath be made known. Pleading, prayers, and fasting were not sufficient ways to make amends; sackcloth and ashes were not accepted as a way to soften God's anger. The only way to appease God is through almsgiving and works of mercy. "Share your bread with the hungry and bring the poor and the homeless into your house. When you see the naked, give them clothing and do not reject your own children. Then your light will break forth as the dawn; you will quickly gain good health; your righteousness will be seen by all and the glory of God will surround you. Then when you cry out, God will answer you, and while you are still asking, he will reply, 'Here I am'" [Isa. 58:7–9].

5. The ways in which we may please God are described for us by God himself: the Scriptures have taught what sinners should do. God is satisfied when we do works of justice, and sins are forgiven through acts of mercy. In Solomon we read, "Store up your alms in the hearts of the poor and they will intercede for you against any evil" [Sir. 29:12], and, "Whoever refuses to hear the cry of the poor will cry to God and not be heard" [Prov. 21:13]. Those who have not shown mercy will not be given mercy by the Lord; those who have not responded to the prayer of the poor will not receive a divine response to their own prayer. In the Psalms the Holy Spirit declares and affirms, "Blessed are those who consider the poor, for the Lord will deliver them when they face trouble" [Ps. 41:1]. Daniel remembered this when King Nebuchadnezzar was in trouble after his frightening dream. In order to seek God's help in averting disaster, he advised the king, "Therefore, O King, listen to my advice; seek forgiveness for your sins by practicing righteousness, and for your gross injustice by showing justice to the oppressed. Then God will give you peace" [Dan. 4:27]. Because the king did not follow this advice, he endured the misfortunes and disasters that he had seen in his dream. He could have avoided and escaped this fate if he had redeemed his sins by giving alms. The angel Raphael teaches the same thing and commands that alms be given freely and in great quantity: "Prayer is good when combined with fasting and almsgiving. Almsgiving preserves one from death and wipes away all sin" [Tobit 12:8–10]. This shows that our prayer and fasting bring better results when combined with almsgiving, and that our

requests to God are granted more fully when they are accompanied by works of mercy and justice. The angel reveals and assures us that our prayers become more efficacious through our almsgiving and that such acts of mercy protect us from dangers and rescue our souls from death. . . .

23. How do we reply to the arguments and excuses of the affluent who refuse to give alms? How can we defend the affluent whose minds are barren and confused? How can we excuse them when we are even lower than the devil's servants and are not willing to repay Christ, even in small ways, for the price of his passion and death? He has given us commands and taught us what we should do. He has promised rewards to those who give and share freely, and he has threatened the unfruitful with punishment. He has made it clear how he will judge humanity and what his final sentence will be. What excuse is left for the lazy? What defense for those whose lives bear no good fruit? If the servant does not do what he is told, he will receive the punishment that was threatened. "When the Son of man comes in glory, and all the angels with him, then he will sit on the throne in glory and the nations will be gathered before him. He will separate them as a shepherd divides the sheep from the goats, and he will place the sheep on his right side and the goats on his left. Then the King will say to those on his right, 'Come. O blessed of my Father, inherit the kingdom prepared for you from the foundation of the world, for I was hungry and you gave me food; I was thirsty and you gave me water; I was a stranger and you accepted me into your home; naked and you gave me clothing; sick and you visited me; in prison and you came to me.' Then the righteous will ask him, 'Lord, when did we see you hungry, thirsty, or naked? When did we see you sick or in prison and come to you?' The King will answer, 'Truly, I say to you, when you did it for one of the least of my children, you did it to me.' [The text from Matt. 25:31–46 continues, concluding: Those failing to do these things] will go away to eternal punishment, but the righteous will enter eternal life."

What greater things could Christ say to us? What better way could he encourage us to works of justice and mercy than to say that such acts are done to himself and that he is offended when we fail to reach out to the poor and needy? Those in the church who are not moved to help a brother or sister may be encouraged when they see how Christ is involved, and those who do not help the suffering may remember that our Lord is in that person who needs our help.

24. Therefore, dear friends, you live with deep reverence for God, and you have rejected the things of the world in order to set your thoughts on things heavenly and divine. Let us offer our complete faith, our devout minds, our obedience, and our continual labors to the Lord that he may be pleased with us. Let us give earthly garments to Christ so that we receive heavenly robes; let us share food and drink in this world so that we may join Abraham, Isaac, and Jacob at the heavenly banquet. So that we do not receive a minimal harvest, let us plant in great quantity. While there is time, let us seek safety and eternal salvation. The apostle Paul says, "While we have the opportunity, let us do good to all people, and especially to those who are of the household of faith. Let us not grow weary of doing good, for in time we shall reap the rewards" [Gal. 6:9–10].

25. We need to remember what the lives of the first believers were like at the time of the apostles. They were filled with great virtues and burned with the warmth of their new faith. They sold their houses and farms and gladly gave all they had to the apostles for distribution to the poor. By freeing themselves and selling their earthly possessions, they transferred their title to the eternal land and its fruits, homes that would be theirs for eternity. This was the reward for their many good works and their unity in love. In the Acts of the Apostles we read, "Now the company of believers acted with one heart and soul, for there was no distinction among them and no one claimed possession of anything, for all was owned in common" [Acts 4:32]. Surely this is the way to become children of God by spiritual birth; this is the way to follow the heavenly law and to imitate the compassion of God the Father. Whatever God has is given to us to use, and no person is denied the opportunity to receive God's blessings and gifts. The light of day, the radiance of the sun, the rain, and the wind are given to all. Everyone shares the same sleep and the beauty of the moon and stars. In the same spirit of equality we on earth share our possessions freely and justly with the community in imitation of God the Father.

26. What then, my dear friends, will be the reward for those who practice charity? The Lord will gather his people and distrib-

ute the rewards he has promised in accordance with their good works and merits. With great and overflowing joy they will receive heavenly gifts for earthly ones, eternal for temporal, and great for small. Our Lord will offer us to the Father as those whom he has restored and sanctified. Through the shedding of his blood we will be raised to eternity and immortality, and paradise will be opened to us. We will enter heaven itself in the faith of his true promises! Think over these things and accept them completely in faith, love them with your whole heart, and let them become alive in your life of continual works of mercy. Those saving works of mercy are a glorious and divine thing, a great comfort to believers, a good way to protect our security, a defense for our hope, a guarding of our faith, the medicine against sin. Such actions are within your power to perform, and they are at the same time great but easy. They offer you a crown of peace without the risk of persecution. They are true and great service of God; they are necessary for the weak, glorious to the strong, a way for the Christian to receive spiritual grace, a positive recommendation for us before Christ the judge, and our way of repaying our debt to God. Let us work willingly and immediately to receive this badge of salvation. As we seek justice and righteousness, let us run with Christ and God watching us, and let us not slacken our pace with desires for this life and this world, for we have now begun a race that is greater than what this world and this office can offer. If the day of reward or of persecution should come, the Lord will not fail to reward the merits of those who have persevered in the race of promoting justice and mercy. In time of peace he gives conquerors the white crown for their labors; in time of persecution we receive a purple crown as a reward for giving our life.

VII.

The Council of Elvira

CANONS

1. A baptized adult who commits the capital crime of sacrificing to the idols is not to receive communion even when death approaches.

2. Flamens who have been baptized but who then offer sacrifices will double their guilt by adding murder (if they organize public games) or even triple it with sexual immorality, and they cannot receive communion even when death approaches.

3. Flamens who have not offered sacrifices but who have presided at public games have kept themselves from complete destruction and may receive communion when death approaches if they have done the required penance. If they commit sexual offenses after completing the penance, they shall be denied any further communion since receiving would make a mockery of the Sunday communion.

4. Flamens who have been catechumens for three years and who have abstained from sacrifices may be baptized.

5. If a woman beats her servant and causes death within three days, she shall undergo seven years' penance if the injury was inflicted on purpose and five years' if it was accidental. She shall not receive communion during this penance unless she becomes ill. If so, she may receive communion.

6. If someone kills another by sorcery or magic, that person shall not receive communion, even at the time of death, for this action is a form of idolatry.

7. If a Christian completes penance for a sexual offense and then again commits fornication, he or she may not receive communion even when death approaches.

8. Women who without acceptable cause leave their husbands and join another man may not receive communion even when death approaches.

9. A baptized woman who leaves an adulterous husband who has been baptized, for another man, may not marry him. If she does, she may not receive communion until her former husband dies, unless she is seriously ill.

10. If an unbaptized woman marries another man after being deserted by her husband who was a catechumen, she may still be baptized. This is also true for female catechumens. If a Christian woman marries a man in the knowledge that he deserted his former wife without cause, she may receive communion only at the time of her death.

11. If a female catechumen marries a man in the knowledge that he deserted his former wife without cause, she may not be baptized for five years unless she becomes seriously ill.

12. Parents and other Christians who give up their children to sexual abuse are selling others' bodies, and if they do so or sell their own bodies, they shall not receive communion even at death.

13. Virgins who have been consecrated to God shall not commune even as death approaches if they have broken the vow of virginity and do not repent. If, however, they repent and do not engage in intercourse again, they may commune when death approaches.

14. If a virgin does not preserve her virginity but then marries the man, she may commune after one year, without doing penance, for she only broke the laws of marriage. If she has been sexually active with other men, she must complete a penance of five years before being readmitted to communion.

15. Christian girls are not to marry pagans, no matter how few eligible men there are, for such marriages lead to adultery of the soul.

16. Heretics shall not be joined in marriage with Catholic girls unless they accept the Catholic faith. Catholic girls may not marry Jews or heretics, because they cannot find a unity when the faithful and the unfaithful are joined. Parents who allow this to happen shall not commune for five years.

17. If parents allow their daughter to marry a pagan priest, they shall not receive communion even at the time of death.

18. Bishops, presbyters, and deacons, once they have taken

their place in the ministry, shall not be given communion even at the time of death if they are guilty of sexual immorality. Such scandal is a serious offense.

19. Bishops, presbyters, and deacons shall not leave the area where they work, or travel in the provinces, in order to engage in profitable ventures. If it is an economic necessity, let them send a son, a freedman, an employee, a friend, or someone else. They should engage only in business activities within their own area.

20. If any clergy are found engaged in usury, let them be censured and dismissed. If a layman is caught practicing usury, he may be pardoned if he promises to stop the practice. If he continues this evil practice, let him be expelled from the church.

21. If anyone who lives in the city does not attend church services for three Sundays, let that person be expelled for a brief time in order to make the reproach public.

22. If people fall from the Catholic church into heresy and then return, let them not be denied penance, since they have acknowledged their sin. Let them be given communion after ten years' penance. If children have been led into heresy, it is not their own fault, and they should be received back immediately.

23. In order to help those who are weak, the rigorous fasting that requires no eating for a whole day shall be dropped during the months of July and August.

24. Individuals shall not be admitted as clergy in a province other than the one where they were baptized. Otherwise their life would not be known by those who examine them.

25. Those who have letters of recommendation referring to them as "confessors" should obtain new letters affirming them as "communicants" instead. Simple people are deceived by the honored title of "confessor."

26. The rigorous form of fasting is to be followed every Saturday. This will correct a mistake in our present practice.

27. A bishop or other cleric may have only a sister or a daughter who is a virgin consecrated to God living with him. No other woman who is unrelated to him may remain.

28. A bishop may not receive the offerings of those who are not allowed to receive communion.

29. Persons who have an erratic spirit shall not have their name added to the list of those making offerings, nor shall they be allowed to exercise any form of ministry in the congregation.

30. Those who sinned sexually as youth may not be ordained as subdeacons. This will guard against their being promoted to higher offices later on. If they have already been ordained, they shall be removed from their office.

31. Young men who have been baptized and then are involved in sexual immorality may be admitted to communion when they marry if they have fulfilled the required penance.

32. Anyone who has fallen into mortal ruin because of sin must seek penance from the bishop and not a presbyter. In extreme illness a presbyter may offer communion or may direct a deacon to do so.

33. Bishops, presbyters, deacons, and others with a position in the ministry are to abstain completely from sexual intercourse with their wives and from the procreation of children. If anyone disobeys, he shall be removed from the clerical office.

34. Candles are not to be burned in a cemetery during the day. This practice is related to paganism and is harmful to Christians. Those who do this are to be denied the communion of the church.

35. Women are not to remain in a cemetery during the night. Some engage in wickedness rather than prayer.

36. Pictures are not to be placed in churches, so that they do not become objects of worship and adoration.

37. Those who have suffered from an evil spirit may be baptized as death approaches. If they have been baptized, they may be given communion. Such people are not, however, to light the church candles in public. If they do so, they are to be denied communion.

38. A baptized Christian who has not rejected the faith nor committed bigamy may baptize a catechumen who is in danger of death, if they are on a sea voyage or if there is no church nearby. If the person survives, he or she shall go to the bishop for the laying on of hands.

39. A pagan who requests the laying on of hands at a time of illness, may receive the imposition of hands and become a Christian if his or her life has been reasonably honest.

40. Landlords may not receive as rent anything that has already been offered to idols. If they do so, they shall be excluded from communion for five years.

41. Christians are to prohibit their slaves from keeping idols in

their houses. If this is impossible to enforce, they must at least avoid the idols and remain pure. If this does not happen, they are alienated from the church.

42. Those with a good reputation who seek to become Christians shall remain as catechumens for two years before being baptized. Should they become seriously ill, they may request and receive baptism earlier.

43. In accordance with the Scripture we shall celebrate Pentecost and not continue the false practice [of celebrating the fortieth day after Easter rather than the fiftieth]. If one does not accept this practice, it will be considered a new heresy.

44. A former prostitute who has married and who seeks admission to the Christian faith shall be received without delay.

45. A catechumen who has stayed away from the church for a long time may be baptized if one of the clergy supports his or her claim to be a Christian, or if some of the faithful attest to this, and it appears that the person has reformed.

46. If a Christian gives up the faith and stays away from the church for a long time, provided he or she has not become an idolater, he or she may be received back and commune after ten years of penance.

47. If a baptized married man commits adultery repeatedly, he is to be asked as he nears death whether or not he will reform should he recover. If he so promises, he may receive communion. If he recovers and commits adultery again, he may not commune again, even as death approaches.

48. Those being baptized are not to place money in the baptismal shell since it seems to indicate that the priest is selling what is a free gift. The feet of the newly baptized are not to be washed by the priests or clerics.

49. Landlords are not to allow Jews to bless the crops they have received from God and for which they have offered thanks. Such an action would make our blessing invalid and meaningless. Anyone who continues this practice is to be expelled completely from the church.

50. If any cleric or layperson eats with Jews, he or she shall be kept from communion as a way of correction.

51. If a baptized person has come from heresy, he must not become a cleric. One who has already been ordained is to be removed from office immediately.

52. Anyone who writes scandalous graffiti in a church is to be condemned.

53. A person who has been excluded from communion for an offense can be readmitted only by the bishop who ordered the excommunication. Another bishop who readmits him or her without obtaining the consent of the first bishop is liable to bring tension among his brothers and may be removed from office.

54. Parents who fail to keep the betrothal agreement and who break their child's engagement are to be kept from communion for three years. If the bride or groom has committed a serious crime, the parents are justified in such an action. If both the bride and groom are involved in the sin, the first rule applies and the parents may not interfere.

55. Priests who continue to wear the secular wreath [as former flamens] but who do not perform sacrifices or make offerings to idols may receive communion after two years.

56. Magistrates are not to enter the church during the year in which they serve as *duumvir* [the government official who presides at public occasions and national feasts].

57. Women and men who willingly allow their clothing to be used in secular spectacles and processions shall be denied communion for three years.

58. In all places, and especially where the bishop resides, those who bring letters indicating their right to commune shall be examined to affirm the testimony.

59. A Christian may not go to the capitol and watch the pagans offer their sacrifices. If a Christian does, he or she is guilty of the same sin and may not commune before completing ten years of penance.

60. If someone smashes an idol and is then punished by death, he or she may not be placed in the list of martyrs, since such action is not sanctioned by the Scriptures or by the apostles.

61. A man who, after his wife's death, marries her baptized sister may not commune for five years unless illness requires that reconciliation be offered sooner.

62. Chariot racers or pantomimes must first renounce their profession and promise not to resume it before they may become Christians. If they fail to keep this promise, they shall be expelled from the church.

63. If a woman conceives in adultery and then has an abortion, she may not commune again, even as death approaches, because she has sinned twice.

64. A woman who remains in adultery to the time of her death may not commune. If she breaks the relationship, she must complete ten years' penance before communing.

65. If a cleric knows of his wife's adultery and continues to live with her, he shall not receive communion even before death in order not to let it appear that one who is to exemplify a good life has condoned sin.

66. A man who marries his stepdaughter is guilty of incest and may not commune even before death.

67. A woman who is baptized or is a catechumen must not associate with hairdressers or men with long hair. If she does this, she is to be denied communion.

68. A catechumen who conceives in adultery and then suffocates the child may be baptized only when death approaches.

69. A married person who commits adultery once may be reconciled after five years' penance unless illness necessitates an earlier reconciliation.

70. A husband who knows of his wife's adultery and who remains with her may not commune even prior to death. If he lived with his wife for a period of time after her adultery and then left her, he may not commune for ten years.

71. Those who sexually abuse boys may not commune even when death approaches.

72. If a widow has intercourse and then marries the man, she may only commune after five years' penance. If she marries another man instead, she is excluded from communion even at the time of death. If the man she marries is a Christian, she may not receive communion until completing ten years' penance, unless illness makes earlier communion advisable.

73. A Christian who denounces someone who is then ostracized or put to death may not commune even as death approaches. If the case was less severe, he or she may commune in less than five years. If the informer was a catechumen, he or she may be baptized after five years.

74. Those who are false witnesses commit a crime and are to be excluded. If their action did not bring about death, and they

explain the reasons for their testimony, they shall be excluded for two years. If their explanation is not accepted by the assembled clergy, they are excluded for five years.

75. If someone falsely accuses a bishop, presbyter, or deacon of a crime and cannot offer evidence, he or she is excluded from communion even at the time of death.

76. If a deacon confesses that he had committed a mortal crime before ordination, he is excluded from communion and must complete three years' penance. If, however, the sin is disclosed by someone else, he must complete five years' penance before being accepted as a layman to receive communion.

77. If a deacon serving a community without a bishop or presbyter baptizes, the bishop shall then give his blessing to those baptized. If someone dies before receiving the blessing, that person is to be regarded as justified by his or her faith.

78. If a Christian confesses adultery with a Jewish or pagan woman, he is denied communion for some time. If his sin is exposed by someone else, he must complete five years' penance before receiving the Sunday communion.

79. Christians who play dice for money are to be excluded from receiving communion. If they amend their ways and cease, they may receive communion after one year.

80. Slaves who have been freed but whose former masters are yet alive may not be ordained as clergy.

81. A woman may not write to other lay Christians without her husband's consent. A woman may not receive letters of friendship addressed to her only and not to her husband as well.

VIII.

Basil the Great

LETTER 22: On the Perfection of the Monastic Life

1. There are many instructions written in the divinely inspired Scriptures that must be put into practice by those who desire to please God. At this time I would like to respond briefly to those specific questions causing problems among you. My words are based on the divinely inspired Scriptures and are stated simply so that they can be easily remembered by those who are too busy to read and also by those who use them to remind others of these obligations.

The Christian's way of thinking should reflect the heavenly calling [Heb. 3:1], and his or her life should be worthy of the gospel of Christ [Phil. 1:27].

The Christian should not be distracted [Luke 12:29] or drawn away from remembering God and God's will and commandments.

The Christian, who goes beyond the [Mosiac] law, should not swear oaths or lie [Matt. 5:20].

You should not speak evil or belittle or argue or try to get even [Rom. 12:19] or repay evil with evil [Rom. 12:17] or become hostile [Matt. 5:22]. Instead, be patient [James 5:8] when under pressure and attempt to confront someone only when it is for that person's own good [Titus 2:15], and not out of your personal vengeance. This is what the Lord desires.

You should not criticize others behind their backs for this is then slander even if it is true [1 Peter 2:1]. You should stay away from those who talk maliciously about others.

You should not be involved in silly talk [Eph. 5:4]. You should not be facetious or encourage frivolity [James 4:9]. Do not waste time in small talk that is of no benefit to your listener and hinders those activities God expects of you [Eph. 5:4]. Therefore, be silent and do not interrupt those who have work to do, but as one who has been tested and given the ability to help others grow in faith, only offer words that edify them so that you do not disappoint the expectations of God's Holy Spirit.

You should not impose yourself on a brother's time in order to talk without having those in charge determine whether it would be pleasing to God and for the good of the community.

You must not become enslaved to wine [1 Peter 4:3] or meat or to the pleasures of eating and drinking [2 Tim. 3:4], for the athlete must exercise complete self-control [1 Cor. 9:25].

Do not take for your personal use what has been given to everyone [Acts 4:32]. But be careful not to allow things that belong to the Master to be forgotten or put aside. You are not your own master, but you have been called by God to be a servant to your brothers in the community [1 Cor. 9:19] and should have regard for them as each of you think and act in your own way [1 Cor. 15:23].

2. Do not complain [1 Cor. 10:10] because you do not have all the things you want or because you are tired of your work, for each case is to be judged by those who decide such things.

There should not be screaming or gestures or acts of temper [Eph. 4:31] or other distractions of the mind that hinder us from knowing God's presence [Heb. 4:13].

Moderate your voice according to the occasion.

Do not respond to others with insolence or contempt [Titus 3:2], but in all circumstances show consideration [Phil. 4:5] and respect to everyone [Rom. 12:10].

Do not give signals with your eye movement or adopt other bodily gestures or motions that annoy your brother or indicate contempt [Rom. 14:10].

You should not seek fashionable clothing and shoes, for this is vanity [Matt. 6:29].

You should seek simple clothing that is needed for the body.

You should not consume things that are unnecessary or extravagant, for this is abuse.

You should not look for honor or claim the place of honor [Mark 9:35]. Instead, you should hold each person as above yourself [Phil. 2:3].

You should not be disobedient [Titus 1:9–10].

Do not sit back and eat the food others provide [2 Thess. 3:10]; you should occupy yourself with those labors for the glory of Christ that you are able to accomplish with fervor [1 Cor. 10:31].

Each one should, with the approval of his superiors and with comprehension and assurance, do all things, even eating and drinking, for the glory of God.

You should not switch from one task to another without the approval of those overseeing the work, unless a sudden situation arises when someone needs help.

You should stay in the place where you have been assigned work and not move around unless those in charge decide someone needs assistance.

You should not be discovered going from one work area to another.

You should not build your life on jealousy and rivalry with others.

3. Do not be envious of someone else's good reputation or delight in that person's shortcomings [1 Cor. 13:6].

In Christ's love you should be concerned and saddened by the failures of your brother and rejoice in his successes [1 Cor. 12:26].

Do not be indifferent to those who are in error or sanction them with your silence [1 Tim. 5:20].

When you admonish someone, do it with compassion [2 Tim. 4:2], motivated by your fear of God and the desire to help the person who is in error.

If you are the one who receives the reprimand or rebuke, willingly take it to heart and consider that it is offered for your benefit and correction.

At the moment when you are accused and are facing both the accuser and others, do not contradict the accuser. If the accusation appears to be unjust, you should meet alone with the accuser and discuss the arguments pro and con.

Everyone should, as much as he is able, offer support to those who have accusations against them.

You should not bear hard feelings against those who have repented of their mistakes but offer them pardon from the depths of your heart [2 Cor. 2:7]. One who claims to have repented of sin should not only be filled with deep sorrow for the mistake committed but should also strive to produce fruits worthy of one who is repentant [Luke 3:8]. When someone has already been reprimanded the first time and forgiven, and then sins again, the severity of the judgment will be worse than the first time [Heb. 10:26–27].

If there is someone who has already been admonished the first and second time [Titus 3:10], persisting in error, it is good if several others will make him feel ashamed by reporting him to the superior [Titus 2:8]. If this does not correct his behavior, let him be cut off from the community as one who brings scandal. He is then "regarded as a pagan and a publican" [Matt. 18:15–17] for the well-being of those who strive to continue in obedience, as it is written, "When the wicked fall, the righteous watch in fear" [Prov. 29:16]. But all should grieve for him, as they would for a limb cut off from their body.

Do not let a conflict between brothers continue past the sunset [Eph. 4:26] lest during the night one of them should die and they must face the inevitable charge on the day of judgment.

You should not put off amending your own life until tomorrow, for the future is not assured and many who make such plans never reach the morrow [Luke 12:40].

Do not deceive yourself by filling your stomach, for it only causes nightmares.

Do not deceive yourself by overworking beyond the limits of necessity, for the apostle says, "If we can have food and clothing, we shall be content" [1 Tim. 6:8]. Abundance that goes beyond necessity looks to others like greed, and greed is condemned as idolatry. [Col. 3:5].

You should not be fond of money or the hoarding of possessions for these things have no purpose [Mark 10:23–24]. You who wish to draw near to God need to accept poverty in all things and be held tightly by the fear of God, as it is said, "Pierce my body with your fear, for I am afraid of your judgments" [Ps. 119:120].

May the Lord help you to receive these words with conviction, and may you show forth for God's glory the fruits of the Spirit as God blesses you and our Lord Jesus Christ assists you. Amen.

IX.

Ambrose of Milan

THE DUTIES OF THE CLERGY

Book I

7. As I write to you, my children, I have deliberately quoted the psalm that the prophet David gave to Jeduthun to sing [Ps. 39]. I trust that you will share my delight in its profound and excellent moral teachings. In our brief look at this psalm we have seen that it encourages patience in remaining silent and in waiting for the appropriate time to speak. In the following verses he shows contempt for wealth. Such virtues are the primary basis for moral perfection. While I was reflecting on this psalm, I decided to write this book regarding duties.

Even though philosophers have written on this subject, such as the Greek Panaetius and his son, and the Latin writer Cicero, I did not consider it out of line to write on the same theme. As Cicero wrote to instruct his son, so I write to teach you, my children. I love you who are united to me in the gospel as much as if you were my true children. Human nature does not make us able to love more deeply than does grace. It is right that we should love those with whom we shall share eternal life more than those we will only know in this world. Many people are corrupt and a shame to their parents, but you we have already chosen to love. The others are loved out of ordinary human feelings, but these do not last or provide a basis for an eternal love. You have been chosen to receive both our great affection and the weight of our love. We test what we love, and we love what we have chosen.

8. Now we join together to look at the idea of duties as I write about it, and we must decide if it is a subject only for the schools of the philosophers or if it is also a theme found in the divine

Scriptures. In a wonderful way the Holy Spirit has directed us to a passage in the gospel appointed to be read today. It appears to be a confirmation that we should write about duty and apply it to the life of Christians. After the priest Zacharias was struck speechless in the temple, it was written, "And when his time of duty was completed, he returned to his home" [Luke 1:23]. We see, therefore, that we may use the term "duty" for ourselves.

This is quite natural since the word "duty," *officium,* is derived from "accomplish," *efficium,* with only one letter changed in order to make a more pleasing sound. Regardless, you should not do anything that is hurtful (*officiant*) to others but only what is productive for all.

9. The philosophers believed that duties involved making a choice between what is honorable and what is ordinary. When the two categories come into conflict, one must decide which is more honorable and which is primarily utilitarian. First, duty is looked at in three ways: by asking what is honest, what is ordinary, and which is greater or less than the other.

These questions are then discussed by examining two duties that are honest or honorable, two that are ordinary, and finally, how we gain the ability to judge between them. The philosophers say that what is honorable involves virtue and an honest life, and that what is ordinary involves the daily concerns of wealth, power, and profit. Our task, they say, is to decide which we will choose [Cicero *De Officiis* I.3, II.3].

As Christians we are concerned only with what is decent and honest, for we are controlled by what is to come rather than by our present situation. Nothing is useful to us unless it helps us gain eternal life, and those things which bring pleasure only for the present time are especially useless. We do not seek the conveniences that possessions and profits bring, for we see these as disadvantages that must be avoided. They become a burden to those who have them, and it is not a great loss when they are gone.

Since we look upon duty quite differently from the philosophers, my writing is worthwhile. They see the opportunities of this life as leading to good, but we see them as creating evil. Those who seek a good life here are tormented hereafter, as we see in the parable of the rich man Lazarus who put up with suffering here and found comfort there [Luke 16:25]. Finally, if you do not wish to read the philosophers' eloquent writings, you may read what I write and be rewarded by the simplicity of the subject itself.

10. The concept of deciding what is "appropriate" is already found in our Scriptures where it is explained and commended. In Greek it is πρέπει. We read, "Praise is appropriate to you, O God, in Zion." In Greek this is Σοὶ πρέπει ὕμνος, ὁ Θεός, ἐν Σιων [Ps. 64:1]. The apostle says, "Teaching what is appropriate to sound doctrine" [Titus 2:1], and, "For it was appropriate that he through whom and for whom all things are created, in bringing many children to glory, should make the one who provides their salvation perfect through suffering" [Heb. 2:10].

Did Panaetius or Aristotle write about duty earlier than David? Even Pythagoras, who lived before Socrates, followed in the footsteps of the prophet David and taught a law of silence. He told his students that they should not speak for five years. David, however, did not want to prohibit using a gift of nature but commended us to choose our words with care. Pythagoras made his rule in order to teach how to speak by not speaking, whereas David encouraged speaking as a means of learning how to speak. How can we learn without practicing or improve without experience?

One who wants to become a soldier must practice daily with his weapons, standing as though confronting an enemy before him. In order to learn how to throw a spear one must practice throwing it and also learn to be attentive in order to avoid the spears thrown by the enemy. If one wishes to pilot a ship on the sea or row a boat, one must first practice on a river. Those who wish to develop a good singing voice must practice in order to develop their voice. Those who wish to win a crown of victory in physical contests must strengthen their muscles by daily practice in the wrestling school and build their endurance with constant exercise.

We are taught this by nature with regard to infants. First they repeat sounds, and then they learn to speak. Those sounds are practice and a way of learning how to form words. Those who want to learn how to speak appropriately do not need to avoid using this gift which nature gives us but need to speak with care, just as guards must exercise a steady vigilance and not fall asleep. All things will be strengthened by proper exercise and practice.

David was not always silent but only at certain times; he did not refuse to speak at other times. He did not speak to his enemies or to sinners who annoyed him. He said, "Like a deaf person he does not speak to those who are untrustworthy and who plot deception, for before them he appears to be deaf and does not open his mouth" [Ps. 38:13–14]. It is also said, "Do not answer a fool with his own lack of good sense, or you will appear to be like him" [Prov. 26:4].

Our first duty is to speak carefully. Such speech becomes a sacrifice of praise to God; reverence is observed when the divine Scriptures are read; parents are honored. I realize that many people talk because they have not learned how to keep silent. It is rare for someone to remain silent when speaking would be to his or her advantage. Discreet persons think before speaking and take into consideration to whom they are speaking as well as the time and place. There is a time for silence and a time for speaking, and we must think before we act. It is excellent when we have the right priority in our duties.

11. Every duty is either "ordinary" or "perfect," a distinction found also in the Scriptures. In the Gospel our Lord said, "'If you want to enter eternal life, keep the commandments.' The young man said, 'Which?' Jesus answered, 'You shall not murder; you shall not commit adultery; you shall not give false testimony; honor your father and mother; love your neighbor as yourself'" [Matt. 19:17–19]. Such matters are ordinary duties for they lack something.

Then the young man said to Jesus, "I have observed all of these things since I was young. What do I still lack?" Jesus said, "If you want to be perfect, go and sell all that you have and give to the poor and you will have treasure in heaven. Come and follow me!" [Matt. 19:20–21]. It is also written that the Lord has commanded us to love our enemies, to pray for those who plot against us, who persecute us, or who spread false scandal about us [Luke 6:27]. We do these things if we want to be perfect as our Father in heaven is perfect. He gives the warmth of the sun to the evil and to the good and makes the whole earth fertile with rain and dew, which are given without distinction. This is what perfect duty is, which the Greeks call κατόρθωμα, for it makes whole all that has been incomplete.

Compassion is an excellent trait because it helps us to be perfect as we imitate the Father's perfection. Nothing commends the

Christian more than compassion—primarily when it is extended to the poor in order to share with them the gifts of nature and the fruits of the earth. Use what you possess to support the poor as partners and sisters and brothers. When you give a silver coin, they receive life; when you offer money, it appears to be a fortune to them. Your coin is all that they possess.

The poor, however, give you even more in return, for they give you your salvation. If you clothe the naked, you are clothed with justice; if you welcome the stranger into your home or help those in need, you are welcomed into the saints' fellowship for eternity. There is no greater gift than that! You sow earthly seeds and reap spiritual rewards. Do you wonder about God's judgment upon holy Job? Look at Job's goodness instead, for he is able to say, "I was an eye for the blind and a foot for the lame. I was a father to the weak and kept them warm with the skins from my lambs. The stranger did not sit outside my house, for my door was open to all who came" [Job 29:15–16]. Those who have never sent a poor person away without help are truly blessed. No one is more blessed than those who understand the needs of the poor and the suffering of the weak and helpless. In the day of judgment such people will receive salvation from the Lord, who will repay them for their compassion. . . .

18. The virtue of modesty is excellent, and pleasant is its graciousness. It reflects not only in what we do but in what we say [Cicero *De Officiis* I.37]. Our words do not fall below good manners or show disrespect. What we believe is reflected in our words. Our moderation compels us to speak in ways that will not offend anyone who hears us. In singing, the first rule is control, and this also applies to us as we begin learning how to sing psalms or hymns or even to speak.

Silence, the foundation of all virtues, is the greatest act of modesty. If it appears to be a sign of childishness or pride, it is criticized, but if it is seen to be true modesty, it brings praise. Susanna was silent when she faced death. She feared the loss of her modesty more than the loss of her life [Sus. 28]. She could speak only to God as she preserved her modesty, and she did not look up at the men nearby, for to do so would have been immodest since they were watching her.

Such praise is not only for chastity, since modesty goes along with innocence, and both protect chastity itself. Restraint is also good as a defender and supporter of chastity, for it keeps one from placing innocence in danger. It is precisely this that first commends the Mother of our Lord to those who read the Scriptures and who see there a true account of why she was chosen for her office. When she was alone in her room, the angel greeted her, and in her uneasiness she remained silent. The Virgin was troubled by the appearance of this stranger, and out of modesty, and not mere shyness, she did not return the greeting. Her only answer was to ask how it was possible that she would conceive and give birth to the Lord. Certainly she did not ask this merely to offer a reply!

Modesty is an important part of our prayers and receives God's grace. Was it not for this reason that the prayer of the tax collector was respected and heard when he could not even lift up his eyes to heaven? He was justified by the Lord's decision, but the Pharisee remained filled with crippling pride [Luke 18:10]. Peter says, "Let us pray with a spirit of imperishable quietness and modesty, for to this God gives much value" [1 Peter 3:4]. Modesty is a great thing, for it does not seek its rights, takes nothing, and claims nothing for itself, but willingly restricts itself and becomes valuable in the sight of God, something nothing else is able to do. Modesty is precious, for it is a part of God. Paul instructs us to pray with modesty and care [1 Tim. 2:9]. This should come first as preparation for our prayers, for the sinner's prayer is not boastful but subdued with shame. The remembrance of our offense leads us to modesty and then to grace.

We must be careful of our modesty in the way we move, gesture, and walk [Cicero *De Officiis* I.35]. What is in our mind is reflected through our body. The inner man hidden in our heart, may be seen to be immature, boastful, or unruly. Or the contrary, we may be respected as one who is stable, dependable, pure, and mature. We must realize that the body is a voice for the soul.

You may remember, my children, that one of our friends who performed his tasks well was nevertheless denied ordination by me because of his exaggerated and unsuitable gestures. I also requested one of our clergy not to walk in front of me, because the sight of his affected stride offended my eyes. I said this to him when he returned to his duties after committing an offense. I would not tolerate such actions, and my judgment has proved correct, for both have left the church. What their mannerisms indicated was substantiated by the unfaithfulness of their hearts. The one abandoned his faith during the Arian difficulties; the other, because he loved money, denied that he was one of us, in order to avoid discipline from the church. In their manner of walking one could see their instability, for they gave the appearance of wandering clowns.

There are some who try to imitate the gestures of actors, and they walk as though carrying items in a procession. They look like moving statues that are following a cadence in their movements.

I do not think that we should walk quickly unless danger or an emergency demands it. We often see people gasping with distorted faces because of their pace. If there is no good reason for such rushing about, it only becomes a cause of offense. I am talking not about those who occasionally need to make haste but about those who have allowed such rapid movement to become an unconscious habit. I do not approve of the very slow, who look like ghosts, nor those in constant rapid motion who look as if a disaster is taking place.

An appropriate stride gives the appearance of authority, stability, and dignity, and reflects tranquillity. It should be simple and natural so that it does not appear to be intentional, conceited, or artificial. Let our movements be natural, and if there are any faults in our nature, correct them diligently. Do not stop correcting your mannerisms.

If we are to pay attention to such outward things, how much more should we be careful of the words that come from our mouths, for they may disgrace us completely. It is not food that contaminates us but the derision of others and obscene words [Cicero *De Officiis* I.37], for such things are openly disgraceful. Those in our office must not let words come out that are indecent and destructive to modesty. And not only should we avoid using shameful language but we should avoid even listening to it. Joseph ran away without his garment in order to avoid hearing that which was detrimental to his modesty [Gen. 39:12].

To have firsthand knowledge of what is indecent is despicable. To watch such a thing, even if unintentionally, is horrible! Can that which we dislike in others be acceptable in ourselves? Do we not learn from nature when we look at the perfection of every part of our body and the way in which everything is functional and adds to its grace and beauty? Those parts that are beautiful to look at are in open view; the head, set above all with its pleasing lines, and the prominent features of the face. And yet each part is also useful! Those parts that relate to natural functions are not prominent but are hidden away in the body itself so that they do not need to be seen. Nature has also taught and persuaded us to cover them. [Cicero *De Officiis* I.35].

Is not nature itself a teacher of modesty? Following nature's example we have learned to be modest, which means to know what is proper, and we have covered and veiled the hidden parts of our body [Cicero *De Officiis* I.40]. It is like the door that Noah was commanded to make in the side of the ark [Gen. 6:16], in which we see a figure of the church and also of the human body. The leftover food was thrown out through that door. Respecting our modesty and guarding what is proper and becoming to our body, nature placed our door for elimination behind us so that it is turned from our sight. Regarding this, the apostle says, "The parts of the body that seem to be weaker are necessary, and those parts of the body that we think are less honorable are the ones to which we show greater honor, and our unseemly parts receive greater modesty" [1 Cor. 12:22–23]. By following nature's example the body's pleasantness has been complemented. In my work *On Noah and the Ark* [chap. 8], I treated this subject more fully and said that we not only hide some parts of the body but also regard it as poor taste to mention their name or describe their function.

If these parts are inadvertently exposed, modesty is violated; but if it is on purpose, it is seen as blatant insolence. Ham, Noah's son, disgraced himself when he saw his father naked and laughed, but those who covered their father received a blessing [Gen. 9:22]. In ancient Rome as well as other countries, it was the custom that grown-up sons not enter the baths with their parents, or sons-in-law with their fathers-in-law, so as not to weaken the respect one has for parents. Many try to cover themselves as much as possible when in the baths and, when they are nude, attempt to cover what is necessary.

We read in Exodus that the priests, under their old law, wore breeches in obedience to the Lord's word to Moses: "You shall make linen breeches to cover their private parts: from the loins to the thighs they shall reach. Aaron and his sons shall wear them when they enter the tent of meeting and when they approach the altar in the holy place to offer sacrifice. If they do not, they will bring guilt on themselves and die" [Exod. 28:42–43]. It is said that some of us still observe this, but most interpret it spiritually and look upon it as a way of protecting modesty and insuring chastity.

19. I have enjoyed being able to spend so much time on the various aspects of modesty, and I speak to you who recognize the value of it for yourselves and not to those condemned by its loss. It applies to all periods of history, all people at any time and in any place, and is especially fitting for the years of childhood and adolescence.

Whatever our age, we must be careful that what we do is fitting and proper and becoming to our whole life. Cicero believes that decorum follows a prescribed order: beauty, order, and the appropriate accouterments for the work to be done. This, he says, is difficult to express in words and yet it can be sufficiently understood [Cicero *De Officiis* I.35].

I do not understand why Cicero included beauty, though he does praise the virtues of the human body. We do not look upon physical beauty as a virtue, but we do not exclude the purity of a blush of modesty. Just as a workman does better with the proper materials, so modesty benefits from the beauty of the body. We do not add such beauty to the body, but it comes naturally and is simple, inherent, and not contrived, not accentuated by expensive, dazzling garments but accompanied with ordinary clothing. We may seek what is basic and necessary, but we add nothing merely for good looks.

The voice should not be dull, weak, or effeminate, a habit many seem to fall into, thinking that it is dignified. The voice should reflect a special quality, rhythm, and virility. All persons should do what is most natural for themselves and their sex and reach their own personal fulfillment. This arrangement enables everyone to be prepared for his or her own work. But I cannot approve of an insipid, weak voice or effeminate gestures, nor can I tolerate those who are ill-mannered or uncouth. Imitate nature; then we will have a rule to guide our actions and a guide for integrity.

20. Modesty involves many rocky places—not inherent in the virtue itself but in the obstacles faced when we encounter those who are dissolute and who use the pretext of enjoyment to poison the good. Those who continue to revel at banquets and games

or join in the sport events will dissipate their manly strength. We must beware that we do not lose all harmony, the blending together of good works, when we attempt to relax our mind. Habit can quickly move nature in another direction.

You would be prudent to do only those things suitable for all clerics and especially those in the highest office of the ministry. Do not attend the banquets of those outside the faith, but continue to show hospitality to the stranger so that no criticism can be made against you. Indeed, such banqueting with non-Christians can become very attractive and soon draw one to a love of feasting. Stories about the world and its pleasures can also have an effect on you, for you cannot keep from hearing them, lest you will appear to consider yourself superior. Your glass is filled repeatedly, even when you object. It is better if you can excuse yourself once and for all time at your own home rather than frequently excusing yourself in the home of others. When you are able to stand up sober, you should not be condemned because of the overindulgence of others.

Younger clergy have no need to visit the homes of virgins or widows except for a pastoral reason, and then they should be accompanied by someone who is older, such as the bishop or, if the matter is quite important, the presbyters. Why should we give the world a chance to criticize? What reason is there to allow frequent visits to become a cause for gossip? What if one of those women yields to temptation? Why should you be implicated in her fall? Many strong men have been overcome by their passions! Many may not have fallen into sin but have lost their credibility!

Why do you not spend your free time from church duties by reading? Why not revisit with Christ, talk with him, and listen to him? We speak to him when we pray, and we hear him when we read the divine writings.

What place do we have in the houses of those outside the Christian community? There is one house, which is for all. Those who need us can come to us. What do we have to do with fictitious stories? We have been called to a ministry before the altar of Christ, not a responsibility to comply with the expectations of others.

We should be humble, gentle, sensitive, stable, and patient. We should be moderate in all things, so that our life does not reflect any flaw through our appearance or the words we speak. . . .

27. Duty springs forth initially from good judgment [Cicero *De Officiis* I.6]. What is greater duty than to direct our attention and reverence to the Creator? From this source other virtues emerge; justice requires good judgment in order to decide what is just or unjust. A mistake either way is very serious. As Solomon says, "One who condemns the righteous or justifies the unrighteous is an abomination to God" [Prov. 17:15]. On the other hand you cannot have good judgment without justice; devotion to God is the beginning of knowledge. We see that this understanding is something the world has borrowed from those who seek such devotion, believing it to be fundamental to all virtues.

Those who love justice must first direct it to God; second, to their country; third, to parents; and last, to all people. This is the way in which nature reflects it. As we begin life and understanding is first revealed to us, we love life as a gift of God; we love our country and our parents; last, we love our peers, who are our companions. From this love develops that which helps us to not look to ourselves but to others. This is the principle behind justice.

By nature every creature will seek, first of all, to find safety and avoid harm and work for its own advantage [Cicero *De Officiis* I.4]. It seeks food and shelter in order to be protected from dangers, storms, and the sun. This is a sign of good judgment. Next we see that creatures are naturally inclined to group together, first with their own kind and then with others. We see cattle and horses in herds, and deer with other deer and, sometimes, with human beings. What can I say about their drive to procreate offspring, or even their mating habits, which reflect a form of justice?

It is apparent that these and the other virtues are all interrelated. Courage reflects justice when it protects one's country in time of war or defends the weak and the oppressed. Good judgment and moderation are not only necessary for discretion but they also guide us in making decisions regarding our actions and our use of time and circumstances. To recognize an opportunity and to use it correctly is justice. In all of this we must remain tolerant and use our strength of body and mind to fulfill the tasks we face.

28. Justice, then, relates to society and the whole human community. That which holds society together is divided into two

parts: justice and humanitarianism (the latter can also be called generosity and kindness) [Cicero *De Officiis* I.7]. It seems to me that justice is the greater but humanitarianism the more pleasant, since the one makes judgment and the other does good works.

The very duty that the philosophers see to be primary to justice, we reject. They say we should hurt no one except when responding to wrongs received. The gospel has taught the opposite. The Scripture teaches that the Spirit of the Son of man should be within us to help us give grace and not harm [Luke 9:56].

The philosophers also believe that justice requires that public property be treated as public and private property as private. But this is not what nature illustrates, for nature has provided all things for common use. God has decreed that all things are produced so that food is available to all and the earth is possessed by everyone equally. Nature provides for everyone, but greed has restricted the supply to only a few. The Stoics taught that all the things the earth produces are for humans to use, and that some people are created to be a benefit to others [Cicero *De Officiis* I.9].

Is this not what Scripture teaches? Moses wrote that God proclaimed, "Let us make humans in our image and likeness, and let them rule over the fish of the sea, the birds of the air, the cattle, and everything that crawls on the earth" [Gen. 1:26]. David said, "God has given dominion over all things: sheep and oxen, wild beasts, the birds in the air, and the fish in the sea" [Ps. 8:6-8]. These philosophers have learned from our writings that all created things are subject to human control and were created to benefit humanity.

In the books of Moses we see the idea that some people are created to be a benefit to others. The Lord says, "It is not good that a man should be alone, so let us make a partner for him" [Gen. 2:18]. Thus woman was created to be a mate for the man and to bear children as a way of helping him. Before the woman was created we are told that "there was no partner found" to be with Adam [Gen. 2:20]. The only mate for a human had to be another human. Among all the creatures there was nothing suitable for him or, more precisely, to be his partner. Therefore a woman was created to be his spouse.

According to God's will and the dictates of nature, we should be of help to one another, even trying to outdo one another in performing good works. Our actions, whether they are the fulfilling of duties, the sharing of money, or the performance of good works, bring blessings to all humanity. We should not be afraid of fulfilling our duties to society whether these bring personal success or failure [Cicero *De Officiis* I.9]. Moses was not afraid to go to war for his people, even against the most powerful kings or the most savage barbarians. He disregarded his own safety for the cause of freeing his people.

The splendor of justice is great. Justice exists for the good of all and helps to create unity and society among us. It is so high that all else must fall beneath its authority, and from it comes help for all and the sharing of monetary contributions. It requires that duty not be neglected even when danger is involved.

Who is not eager to reach the heights of this virtue but held back by selfishness which weakens its power [Cicero *De Officiis* I.7]? When our goal is to make money and accumulate possessions, to buy more land and be the richest of all, we have rejected the virtue of justice and are not able to be a blessing to others. How can you be just if you attempt to add to yourself what you take from others?

The desire for power destroys the beauty and virility of justice [Cicero *De Officiis* I. 8]. Can one who seeks to subdue some be an advocate for others? How can someone help the weak against the powerful while aspiring to power at the expense of others' liberty?

29. We realize how great justice is when we see that no place, no person, no time period has ever been without it. It must be acknowledged in dealing with enemies—for example, by not moving onto the battlefield or beginning to fight before the time that has already been agreed upon by both sides [Cicero *De Officiis* I.11]. It is understood that some will lose battles because of their weakness or their opponents' skill, or even because of luck. A greater revenge is shown against those who have been barbaric, dishonest, or cruel, such as the Midianities [Numbers 31]. They used their women to cause the people of Israel to sin, and the Lord's anger was upon the people of our fathers. When Moses won the battle, he did not allow the women to live. The Gibeonites, however, who deceived the people of our fathers rather than fight them, were not attacked by Joshua but were allowed to

become servants [Joshua 9]. Elisha did not permit the king of Israel to kill Syrians but instead commanded that their soldiers, who were attacking the city, be struck with momentary blindness so that they could not see their way; they were then led into the city. Elisha then said, "You shall not slay them since you have not taken them captive with your sword and spear. Give them bread and water and let them eat and drink and return to their own master" [2 Kings 6:22]. They showed to others the same kindness which they had received. "And the Syrians did not come again to raid the land of Israel" [2 Kings 6:23].

If justice is binding in a time of war, should it not be even more so in time of peace? The prophet showed such mercy to those who came to seize him. We are told that the king of Syria sent his army to capture Elisha, who had made the king's plans and deliberations known to all. When Gehazi, Elisha's servant, saw the army, he cried out in fear for his own life, but the prophet said to him, "Fear not. Those on our side are greater in number than those on their side" [2 Kings 6:16]. When the prophet prayed that his servants' eyes would be opened, they were opened and Gehazi saw that the mountain was full of horses and chariots surrounding Elisha. When the army came near, the prophet prayed, "O God, strike the Syrians with blindness." After this was answered he said to the Syrians, "Follow me and I will take you to the man you seek." Then they saw Elisha, the man they were seeking, but they could not capture him [2 Kings 6:8–23]. It is clear from this passage that faith and justice should be preserved even in time of war, for it would be a disgrace if faith were disregarded.

People in the past tried to give their enemies a less harsh name by calling them strangers [Cicero *De Officiis* 1.12]. The ancient custom was to refer to enemies as strangers. Such a custom was taken from our writings, for we see that the Hebrews referred to their enemies as *allophyllos*, or in Latin, *alienigenas*, "aliens." In 2 Kings we read, "It came about in those days that aliens came to fight against Israel."

The foundation of justice is faithfulness. The hearts of the just concentrate on faith, and when they look at themselves, they build justice upon their faith, and this justice is apparent when they speak the truth. The Lord said through Isaiah, "Behold, I am laying a foundation stone in Zion" [Isa. 28:16]. This means that

Christ is the foundation of the church. The faith of all is centered in Christ, and the church is the living manifestation of justice, which is shared with all. The church prays for all, works for all, and shares the struggle of all who face temptation. Those who deny themselves are just and worthy of Christ. Because of this, Paul looks to Christ as the foundation upon whom we base works of justice that arise from faith. Injustice comes from our works if they are evil, but justice comes from works that are good. . . .

35. We have discussed the nature and power of virtues based on justice [Cicero *De Officiis* I.18]. Now we look at courage, which, being so important, must be divided into two parts: courage in war and courage at home. The area related to war is alien to our office, and we must be concerned with things of the soul and not of the body. We concern ourselves not with weaponry but with peace. Some of our ancestors, however, received glory in battle: Joshua, the son of Nun, Jerubbaal, Samson, and David.

Courage is a virtue exceeding the others, but it must never be seen alone. It cannot remain by itself since courage without justice leads to injustice [Cicero *De Officiis* I.19]. The stronger the courage, the more temptation there is to oppress the weak; and when it comes to battle, the war must be judged as either just or unjust.

David went to war only out of necessity. His good judgment was combined with his courage in battle. When he faced the giant Goliath for single-handed combat, he refused to wear the armor that hindered him. His own strength was more important than the weapons of others. From a distance he was able to throw a stone with much force, and the enemy was slain [1 Sam. 17:39]. From that time on he never entered battle without seeking guidance from the Lord [1 Sam. 5:19]. Therefore he triumphed in battle even into old age, when, in war with the Philistines, he entered battle seeking further honor and neglected his own safety [1 Sam. 21:15].

There are other kinds of courage that are important too. We praise the courage of those who "through faith muzzled the mouths of lions, quenched the raging fire, escaped the sharp sword, and gained strength out of weakness" [Heb. 11:33–34]. Their victory came not in the midst of an army but in the battle that they fought completely alone. Their triumph came from their own courage. How insurmountable Daniel was when he did not fear the lions that surrounded him! While the lions roared, he was eating.

36. The glory of courage lies not in the strength of one's body or arms but in the excellence of one's mind [Cicero *De Officiis* I. 23]. Not to cause injury but to guard against it is the law of courage. Those who do not, as much as they are able, fight against what harms a friend are as much at fault as those who cause the injury. This was the first example of courage we see in regard to holy Moses. When he saw a Hebrew being injured by an Egyptian, he befriended him, killed the Egyptian, and hid his body in the sand [Exod. 2:11–12]. In addition, Solomon said, "Rescue those who are being led away to death" [Prov. 24:11].

It is therefore apparent where Cicero, Panaetius, and Aristotle got their ideas. Before they were alive, Job had said, "I delivered the poor out of the hand of the strong and the fatherless who had no one to fight for them. May the blessing of those who were about to perish come upon me" [Job 29:12–13]. Was not Job extremely brave when he withstood the power of the devil and defeated it with the strength of his own will? We should not doubt the courage of those to whom the Lord said, "Take hold of yourself and be a man; be resolute and strong. All who cause injury are humbled" [Job 40:2]. The apostle says, "You have strong encouragement" [Heb. 6:18]. Those who find consolation in grief are brave.

It is quite fitting to call persons courageous when they conquer themselves and control anger, refuse temptation, remain resolute in misfortune, do not become conceited with success, and do not get carried away by every change that takes place [Cicero *De Officiis* I.20]. What is more excellent or splendid than training one's mind to control the body and to subjugate it to rational reasoning so that it will carry out the intentions and desires of the mind?

Courage of the mind is seen in two ways: first, it is the ability to see outward goods as unimportant and superfluous, and not to seek them; and second, it is to seek with all one's strength those things which are seen to be proper or, as the Greeks say, πρέπει [Cicero *De Officiis* I.20]. What is more important than to train one's mind not to place a high value on possessions, pleasures, and honors, or to spend much time in seeking such things? We must learn to concentrate our mind on things that are useful and suitable. When our lives focus on such things, the sudden loss of property, the lack of worldly recognition, and the rebuff of unbelievers will not affect us or be of concern. Even the dangers we face for the cause of justice will not hinder us.

This is the true courage that Christ's athlete has when competing for the crown according to the rules [2 Tim. 2:5]. Do you think the example of courage is weak when we read, "Sufferings bring endurance; and endurance, experience; and experience produces hope" [Rom. 5:3–4]. There are many contests but only one trophy! That victory comes only to those who were strengthened by Christ Jesus and who pushed themselves without resting. "There is affliction on all sides, fighting without and fear within" [2 Cor. 7:5]. In danger, in constant labor, in prison, and near to death, his mind was not changed and he continued on, becoming stronger because of his weakness [2 Cor. 11:24].

Consider how his example applies to us who hold offices in the church. We must reject earthly possessions, for "if you died with Christ to the elemental spirits of the world, why do you live as though you belong to the world? Do not touch, or taste, or use those things that perish as they are used" [Col. 2:20–22]. Scripture also says, "If you have been raised with Christ, seek those things above and not the things of the earth" [Col. 3:1–2]. Also, "Put to death the parts of you that belong to the earth" [Col. 3:5]. This applies to all Christians, but you, my child, he commands to reject wealth and avoid pagan teachings and superstitious fables. Instead, you shall "train yourself in goodness, for bodily exercise is of limited value, but holiness is profitable in all ways" [1 Tim. 4:8].

Let your holiness lead you to justice, continence, and gentleness, and flee from childish actions so that, grounded and rooted in grace, you may achieve the good faith. "Do not become entangled in secular affairs, for you are fighting for God" [2 Tim. 2:4]. A soldier of the emperor is forbidden, according to human law, from engaging in legal matters, selling merchandise, or taking part in the business of the marketplace. Is it not more important for those who are soldiers of the faith to keep away from all manner of worldly business and to be content with their own small farm, if they have one? If you do not have one, be content with the pay you receive for your work. It is well said in the words, "I have been young and now am old, yet I have not seen those who are righteous forgotten or their children **begging bread**" [Ps. 37:25]. Here we have the true peace and moderation of mind that is not afflicted by the desire for gain or the fear of loss.

Book II

1. In the first book we discussed the duty that is required for an honorable life, a life understood to be blessed, for as Scripture says, it leads to eternal life. The splendor of an honorable life is reflected in the blessings of a peaceful conscience and the security of innocence. Just as the rising sun hides the moon and the stars, so a virtuous life outshines all the earthly things and human desires that the world considers to be good and important.

Those are blessed who are judged not according to outside criteria, but according to their inward understanding and feelings. We do not need popular opinion to reward us, nor do we plead out of fear. The less we value honor, the more we will be able to dispense with it. Those who seek for honor in this life will see only a shadow of what is to come, and they will be hindered in reaching eternal life, for Scripture says, "Truly I say to you, they have received their reward" [Matt. 6:2]. This judgment is on those who sound a trumpet to let the world know they have helped the poor. It also applies to those who fast for outward show: they "have their reward."

Therefore, an honorable life requires compassion and fasting performed in secret, for you are seeking God's reward and not the praise of others. Those who seek worldly praise have their reward, but those who seek God's reward will have the eternal life that only he can give. It is said, "Truly, I say to you, today you will be with me in paradise" [Luke 23:43]. In this passage Scripture calls us to a blessed, eternal life. It is not a human opinion but a divine judgment. . . .

30. My children, avoid those who are evil and watch out for those who are envious. There is a difference between the evil and the envious. The evil consider only their own welfare, and the envious despise the good that comes to others. The former love evil, and the latter despise what is good. Those who seek good only for themselves are more tolerable than those who seek evil for everyone.

My children, think before you act, and give much thought before doing what you consider appropriate. If the opportunity to die worthily comes, accept it willingly. Such honor flies away quickly and does not readily offer itself again.

Love faith, for it was his faith and devotion that brought Josiah great love from his enemies [2 Kings 23:21]. He celebrated the Passover of the Lord when he was only eighteen years old, an action not performed previously. His zeal was greater than that of his predecessors, and you, my children, are called to the same zeal for God. Your devotion to God should fill you and devour you so that you may proclaim, "Zeal for your house has consumed me" [Ps. 69:9]. One of Christ's disciples was called a Zealot [Luke 6:15]. Why do I speak about an apostle? The Lord himself said, "Zeal for your house will consume me" [John 2:17]. Your devotion must be to God and not to the world, for that would lead to jealousy.

The peace that surpasses understanding must be among you. Love one another. Nothing is sweeter than charity or more satisfying than peace. You know that I have chosen you and loved you above all others. You are the children of one Father and united in one family.

Hold to what is good, and the God of peace and love will be with you in our Lord Jesus, to whom is honor, glory, praise, and power with the Holy Spirit now and forever. Amen.

Book III

2. We have already spoken about the two questions, What is honorable? and, What is useful? Now we must ask if the two may be compared and which one we should follow. We have already discussed what is honest and what is evil, and we have seen what is useful and useless. Now we must decide what is honorable or merely utilitarian.

I need to do this so that they are not seen as two opposites, since I have argued that they are one and the same. Nothing can be honorable if it is not useful, and nothing is truly useful unless it is also honest. We do not use the logic of the world, which says one should accumulate wealth, but we follow God's wisdom, which counts as valueless the possessions of this world.

This κατόρθωμα, duty fulfilled with perfect honesty, begins with true virtue [Cicero *De Officiis* III.3]. From this follows ordinary duty, which requires no special or difficult virtue but is possible for all. A familiar example is the saving of money; another is the enjoyment of a festive and eloquent banquet. Fasting and moderation are observed, however, by only a few, and those who have no envy are rare. On the other hand, there are many who attempt to take from others and who are not content with what they have. The primary duties are observed by a few, but the ordinary by many.

We frequently use the same words but with different meanings. We call God good, and also man good. In each case "good" has a different meaning [Cicero *De Officiis* III.4]. This is also true when we use the term "wise" to describe God or a person. In the gospel we read, "You must be perfect, as your Father in heaven is perfect" [Matt. 5:48]. I also read that Paul was both perfect and imperfect, for he said, "Not that I have already attained or become perfect, but I continue to try to attain it." He immediately adds, "Therefore, we who are perfect . . ." [Phil. 3:12, 15]. Perfection has two levels, one that is ordinary and related to this life, and the other of a higher rank and related to the life to come. The first is within human potential, but the second is perfection of the future life. God, however, remains just and wise and perfect in all things.

There is a difference among people, as we see when it was said of Daniel, "Who can be wiser than Daniel?" [Ezek. 28:3]. He was wiser than others, just as Solomon possessed wisdom greater than all the wisdom of old or of the wise men of Egypt [1 Kings 4:29–30]. There is an ordinary wisdom shared by many, but only a few have perfect wisdom. Many have the ordinary wisdom related to earthly affairs and how to gain what one wants from another. Those who have perfect wisdom seek things for themselves not in this life but in eternity, and they do what is fitting and honorable not for their own good but to benefit all.

This then is our rule, so that we do not choose wrongly between what is honorable and what is useful. If we are just, we must not take away from someone else and we must not use our power to profit from those who are less powerful. The apostle teaches, "All things are lawful, but not all things are useful; all things are lawful, but not all things help to build up. Let no one seek his own good, but that of his neighbor" [1 Cor. 10:23–24]. This means that we work not for our own benefit or honor but for that of our neighbor. It is also said, "Look upon others as superior to yourself, and look not only to your own interests but to the needs of all" [Phil. 2:3–4].

Do not seek honor or praise for yourself but seek it for others. We see this commended in Proverbs when the Holy Spirit says through Solomon, "My son, if you are wise, use your wisdom for yourself and for those around you; if you are evil, you alone must bear the evil" [Prov. 9:12]. The wise share their wisdom with others as just people who reflect both virtues.

X.

Augustine of Hippo

LETTER 189: To Boniface

1. I had already written a reply to your letter, but before I was able to send it to you, I heard that my dear son Faustus would stop here on his way to visit you. After he was given the letter that I wanted him to bring to you, he informed me that you had requested that I send some personal advice to help you as you seek eternal salvation in your hope through our Lord Jesus Christ. Even though I am quite busy right now, he insisted that I take time because of his deep concern and love for you. I have given in to him and written a rather hasty response in order not to disappoint you, my distinguished and honorable son.

2. In brief, my response is summed up in the words: "Love the Lord your God with all your heart, and with all your soul, and with all your strength; and love your neighbor as yourself" [Matt. 22:37–39]. These are the words our Lord used on earth when he summed up the faith in the gospel: "On these two commandments hang all the law and the prophets" [Matt. 22:40]. You should grow each day in this love both by prayer and by good works, so that he may help and guide you in this gift he gives you, and bring it to perfection in your life. This is the love, the apostle says, that is "placed in our hearts by the Holy Spirit which is given to us" [Rom. 5:5]; it is this love that is the "fulfilling of the law" [Rom. 13:10]; and it is the same love that makes faith work, for he says, "Neither circumcision nor uncircumcision avails anything, but faith, which works by love" [Gal. 5:6].

3. It is in this love that all our holy ancestors, patriarchs, prophets, and apostles pleased God. In this love all true martyrs came up against the devil and gave their lives, and because it did

not grow cold or weaken in them, they were victorious. In this love all true believers make daily progress, not toward an earthly kingdom but toward the heavenly kingdom, not to a temporal but to an eternal inheritance, not gaining gold and silver but gaining the incorruptible riches of the angels, not seeking the possessions of the good life of this world—which bring insecurity and cannot be taken with us when we die—but seeking the vision of God. This vision brings grace and a peace that transcends the beauty of creatures on earth and even in heaven; it is greater than the loveliness of even the greatest saints; it exceeds the glory of the angels and heavenly powers; it excels what language can express or the mind can comprehend. We do not need to give up hope as we seek this wonderful promise, but rather we need to have the faith that we will achieve it because he who promised it is exceedingly great. The apostle John said, "We are the children of God and we do not yet know what we shall be, but we do know that when he appears, we shall be like him, for we will see him as he is" [1 John 3:2].

4. You do not need to fear that someone in military service will be unable to please God. David was in the military, and God blessed him as well as many other soldiers in that time. The centurion came to the Lord and said, "I am not worthy that you should come to my home, but if you will only say the word my servant will be healed. I am a man subject to authority and also having soldiers under me. I say to one, 'Go,' and he goes, or to another, 'Come,' and he comes. To my servant I say, 'Do this,' and it is done." Our Lord said to that centurion, "I say to you that I have yet to find such great faith in Israel" [Matt. 8:8–10]. There also was Cornelius, to whom an angel brought the message "Cornelius, your prayer is heard and your offerings accepted" [Acts 10:1–8]. The angel then sent him to the apostle Peter for advice as to what he should do, but Cornelius sent a devout soldier in his place. There also were soldiers who came seeking baptism from John, the holy forerunner of our Lord and the friend of the bridegroom who said of him, "No one has been born of women who is greater than John the Baptist" [Matt. 11:11]. When the soldiers asked John what they should do, he said, "Do violence to no one, do not accuse others falsely, and be content with your wages" [Luke 3:12–14]. You see, he did not order them to give up their

military careers, but rather he told them to be content with their salaries.

5. Those who give up all worldly activities and accept the life of disciplined chastity have the highest place before God. "Everyone has a special gift from God, one of one kind and one of another" [1 Cor. 7:7]. Some of these Christians pray for you that your invisible enemies might be defeated, and you in turn fight for them as you fight against their visible enemies, the barbarians. How I wish that there could be one faith for all of us so that we would not struggle among ourselves but would conquer the devil and his angels! But it is a part of this life that citizens of the heavenly kingdom must face temptations in the midst of our erring and godless society in order to be tested and "purified as gold in the furnace" [Wisd. of Sol. 3:5–6]. We need to be patient and not wish that we were surrounded only by holy and righteous people, for this reward will come in its own time.

6. When you are preparing for a battle, remember this fact: even your bodily strength is a gift of God, and therefore you must not use this gift of God against God. When you make a pledge, it must be kept even if it is with the enemy you fight, and even more important, if it is with a friend for whom you are going to battle. Your primary aim should be peace; war should be fought only out of necessity in order to ensure that God will remove the cause and allow all to live in peace. Peace is not used as a pretext for stirring up war, but war is waged as a means of securing peace. You must be a peacemaker, even when you go to war, and help those whom you defeat to know the importance of maintaining peace, for our Lord says, "Blessed are the peacemakers, for they shall be called the children of God" [Matt. 5:9]. We must remember, however, that if peace among men is sweet as a way of bringing temporal welfare, how much sweeter is that divine peace which brings eternal happiness with the angels. Only allow necessity, and not your own will, to kill the enemy who fights against you. Just as violence is used against those who rebel and resist, so mercy must be shown to those who have been defeated or captured, especially when they pose no threat to the future peace.

7. Adorn your life with chastity in marriage and with sobriety and moderation, for it is a disgrace if lust defeats one whom others could not conquer, or if wine overpowers one whom the sword could not destroy. If you do not possess worldly riches, do

not try to obtain them through evil actions; if you do possess them, let them be stored up in heaven by your good works. A mature Christian soul should not rejoice in obtaining rich possessions or be crushed when they are lost. Think of what the Lord said: "Where your treasure is, there your heart will be also" [Matt. 6:21]. Surely, when we hear, "Lift up your hearts," we know that our response must be given in unreserved honesty.

8. I know that you have been very careful in these matters, and I rejoice in the good reports that I hear of you. I send my congratulations in the Lord. Let this letter become a mirror for you so that you may see yourself as you are, rather than letting it become a set of instructions to tell you what you ought to be. If, in reading this letter or Holy Scripture, you discover things you lack in leading a holy life, immediately resort to prayer, and pursue that which you are missing. Give thanks to God who is the fountain of goodness for all things that you have, and in all your good deeds give God the glory and keep the humility for yourself. It is written, "Every good gift and every perfect gift is from above and comes from the Father of lights" [James 1:17]. No matter how much you advance in the love of God and of your neighbor, or in true piety, do not get the idea that you no longer sin in this life, for as Scripture says, "Is not our life on earth a life of temptation?" [Job 7:1]. Consequently, as long as you are in this body, you need to pray as our Lord taught us: "Forgive us our sins, as we forgive those who sin against us" [Matt. 6:12]; you must forgive quickly those who have sinned against you and who have asked your forgiveness, so that you may then pray this prayer in honesty and thereby receive forgiveness for your own sins.

I have written this letter to you in haste, dear friend, in order to have it ready before the messenger departs. I am thankful to God that in some manner I have been able to answer your worthwhile request. May God's mercy protect you always, my noble lord and justly distinguished son.

LETTER 220: To Boniface

1. I have never found a more trustworthy man, or one who could get to you more easily with my letters, than the servant and minister of Christ, the deacon Paul, a friend very dear to both of us. Because the Lord has brought him to me at this time, I have an

opportunity to send you a letter, not about the power and honor you have in this evil world, nor about the state of your corruptible and mortal body—because it will someday pass away and we do not know when that will happen—but about the salvation that Christ has promised us. It was for this salvation that he was despised and crucified—in order to show us that we should despise rather than desire the good things of this world. Instead, we should desire and hope for that life which he revealed in his resurrection, for he rose again from the dead and will die no more, for "death shall have no power over him" [Rom. 6:9].

2. I know that you have many friends who are devoted to you in this life and who seek to give you advice that is sometimes useful and sometimes the opposite. They are only human, and therefore they can only see what is known today, for the future is unknown to them. It is not easy for someone to give advice concerning God, or to save your soul from damnation—not because you do not have friends to do this but because it is difficult for them to find an opportunity to discuss such matters with you. I have always wished I could do so, but have never found the time or the place where I could share with the man I love deeply in Christ. You know how bad it was when you honored me with your visit to Hippo! I was so tired and exhausted that I could barely carry on a conversation. Now, my son, listen to me while I speak to you in this letter, a message I was afraid to send you in your time of danger for fear that the messenger would be in danger or that it would fall into the hands of the wrong persons. I ask that you forgive me if you think I have been overly cautious. However that may be, I must admit that it was true.

3. Listen to me, or rather, listen to the Lord our God who speaks through me, his feeble servant. Remember the kind of person you were when your first wife, of hallowed memory, was still living. Just after her death you reacted against the vanity of this world and thought about entering the service of God [as a monk]. I remember well what you said to us at Tubunae about your feelings and hopes when you talked with brother Alypius and me. I am certain that the pressure of present-day worldly activities has not removed the memory of that conversation from you. At that time you wanted to give up all of your public business and to withdraw into a sacred retreat to live as a servant of God in the

monastic life. Why did you not go ahead and do it? Perhaps it was our emphasis upon the benefit your work at that time would bring to the churches of Christ as you concentrated on defending them from the barbarian armies in order that they could "lead a quiet and peaceable life in all piety and chastity" [1 Tim. 2:2]. We also stressed that you should not seek more from this world than that which is necessary to support yourself and your household and that you should practice perfect self-restraint in chastity and put on over your military uniform the stronger armor of the Spirit.

4. While we rejoiced over your decision, you went off on a voyage and married a second wife. Your voyage was in obedience to what the apostle calls the higher powers [Rom. 13:1], but you would not have remarried if you had not been overcome by desire and given up your desire for continence. I was overcome with amazement when I first heard this news, but I received some consolation in the fact that you refused marriage until she became a Catholic. Regardless of that demand, you have allowed the heresy of those who deny the true Son of God [Arianism] to enter your home, and your daughter has been baptized by them. Rumors have reached us—and I hope they are false!—that even some maidens who were dedicated to God have been rebaptized by these heretics. With floods of tears we weep over this great disaster! People are even saying that your wife cannot satisfy your sexual desires and that you defile yourself by having intercourse with concubines. This may be pure slander on their part.

5. What can I say about such great and numerous evils that are common knowledge and that seem to stem from your remarriage? You are a Christian and have a conscience. You fear God. Take a good look at yourself and see the many things that I hesitate to mention and for which you should seek penance. I believe that the Lord is at present sparing you from all dangers so that you have the opportunity to do penance as you should. Listen to what is written: "Do not delay in turning to the Lord, and do not put it off day after day" [Eccles. 5:8]. You claim that there is good reason for what you have done, but I cannot judge your explanation since I do not know all sides in the argument. Whatever your reason, which we do not need to analyze at this moment, can you face God and deny that you are in this predicament because you

loved the things of the world, which, being God's servant, you knew you should despise and reject completely? You may accept what is offered to you and use it to please God; but you must not covet what you have not received or what is entrusted to your care. This craving has brought on your present problems while you love vanity and cause evil—evil not just done by you but, often, done because of you. Some things are feared because they hurt for a brief time when they are done; other things are done that hurt for eternity.

6. To point to one of these things: Who can help seeing the many persons who stay beside you to protect your power and your personal safety? They may be faithful to you and trustworthy, but do they not desire certain advantages in life that you can give them? Their desire comes not from a godly but from a worldly motive. You, as one who satisfies the worldly desires of others, should also curb and control your own desires. To satisfy others, many things must be done that are displeasing to God. Yet, even then, such covetousness is not satisfied, for it is easier to abolish it completely in those who love God than it is to satisfy it even partially in those who love the world. For this reason Scripture says, "Do not love the world, nor things of the world. If anyone loves the world, the love of God is not in that person; for all that is in the world, the lust of the flesh, the lust of the eyes, and human pride, comes not from God but from the world. And the world passes away, and the lust in it, but those who do the will of God abide forever, just as God abides forever" [1 John 2:15–17]. Since you are surrounded by armed men, whose passions must be humored and whose cruelty is feared, how can you ever fulfill—or even partially satisfy—the desires of such men who love the world, without losing everything or without doing what God forbids and what will be punished in eternity? Because of this evil desire there is so much destruction around us that one can scarcely find anything, no matter how worthless, that is left for the plunderer to carry away.

7. What shall I say about the devastation in Africa at this time which is inflicted by African barbarians who have no one to drive them off because you are too busy with your personal problems and have not taken steps to stop this disaster? Who would ever have believed or feared that the barbarians could do so much

widespread damage, or advance so far, or loot so much, or make such vast areas, which were once densely populated, virtual deserts? There was no such fear when Boniface became a count of the Empire and of Africa, with a great army and power! As a tribune he had been able to use his small forces to keep these barbarians subdued out of fear. Everyone expected that you as count would use your authority to subjugate the African barbarians and to make them subjects of the Roman Empire. You can see how such hopes have been dashed! In fact, I do not need to say any more. You can add much more as you reflect on the subject yourself!

8. Perhaps you seek to defend yourself by laying blame on those who have injured you or who have failed to recognize the goals you have accomplished and who have merely concentrated on criticizing. I am unable to look into or judge such arguments. You must look into the matter and analyze the situation since it deals with your relationship to God and not to men. If you are a believer in Christ, you must seek not to offend him. I am concerned with much more important issues and believe that people must see Africa's great calamities as a result of their own sins. I do not, however, want you to become one of those wicked and evil men whom God uses to inflict worldly punishments on some people, for such wicked people will eventually receive eternal punishment unless they amend their lives. Turn your thoughts to God and contemplate the great blessings you have received from Christ, who endured great suffering. Those who wish to be a part of his kingdom and to live in eternal peace with him love their enemies, do good to those who hate them, and pray for those who persecute them [Matt. 5:44]. If on occasion they happen to be overly harsh in disciplining someone, they do not lose the sincere love they have for others. If earthly and transitory benefits have been given to you by the Roman Empire—remember that it is itself an earthly power and cannot dispense heavenly benefits—you must not return evil for good nor can you repay evil with evil. Which of these two may have happened in your case, I am not willing to discuss, nor do I wish to judge. I speak to a Christian: Do not return evil for good nor evil for evil.

9. Perhaps you respond, "What should I do in such a mess?" If you want me to offer advice regarding your worldly life, specifi-

cally, how you can remain safe from harm and hang on to your power and wealth or even increase them, I must admit that I have no answer, because so much of life is uncertain. If, however, you ask me about your relationship to God and how to gain salvation, I have much to say. Fear the word of truth that says, "What profit is it to one who gains the whole world but who suffers the loss of the soul?" [Matt. 16:26]. I have advice for you to follow. There is nothing more important than what I have already said: "Do not love the world nor the things of the world. If anyone loves the world, the love of God is not in that person, for all that is in the world is the lust of the flesh, the lust of the eyes, and human pride, which comes not from God but from the world. And the world passes away and the lust in it, but those who do the will of God abide forever, just as God abides forever" [1 John 2:15–17]. That is my advice! Take hold of it and do it! Prove that you are a strong man! Take control over the desires that make you love the world; do penance for your past evil, which resulted from the control your passions had over you. If you accept my advice, do not forget it, but continue to follow it. If you do, you will obtain the blessings that are promised, and you will pass through the uncertainties of life without losing your salvation.

10. Perhaps you pursue the matter further and ask me how things can happen while you are so entangled in problems. Pray earnestly, and offer to God the words of the Psalm, "Deliver me from my distresses" [Ps. 25:17], for your problems will cease when your passions are under control. He who has heard your prayer, and our prayer on your behalf, that you be delivered from the dangers of visible wars in which the body may be killed (for it will end sometime, but the soul will live on unless it is captive to evil passions) will himself grant you an invisible and spiritual victory over the interior and invisible enemies that are your passions. You will be able to use this world and yet not be subject to it, for with its good things you will do good instead of evil. Such things are good in themselves and are not given to us except by God who has power over all things in heaven and on earth. His gifts are given to the good so that they will not be considered evil; and they are given to the evil so that in themselves they are not seen as being the supreme good. At times they are taken away from the good in order to test them, and from the evil in order to punish them.

11. Who is so foolish as not to understand that physical health in our mortal bodies, victory over our enemies, temporal power and honor, and other earthly goods are all given equally to both good and bad people but taken away from both as well? Your salvation, the immortality of the body, the power of justice, the ability to control our destructive passions, and glory, honor, and eternal peace are given only to the good. You must love these things, earnestly desire them, and seek for them by every possible means. In order to gain such things and to keep them you must give alms, pour out your prayers, fast as much as is possible without impairing your health, and not love earthly possessions regardless of how many surround you. Use your possessions to do many good things and do not do evil because of them. All of these things will someday perish, but good works, even those accomplished by using the perishable possessions of the world, will never perish.

12. If you had not remarried, I would repeat what we said to you at Tubunae, that is, that you should now live in chastity and complete continence. At that time we encouraged you not to give up your military career, but now I believe that you need to withdraw from military duties but not beyond the point where society would be at risk. Devote your time to that life which you wanted, a life in the community of the saints who wage war in silence as soldiers of Christ, not killing others but fighting against "principalities and powers and the spirits of wickedness" [Eph. 6:12]—the devil and his angels. The saints conquer enemies that are unseen, yet they are victorious because they subjugate the objects of their senses. I cannot urge you to follow that life, because you now have a wife and it would be wrong for you to live under a vow of continence without her agreement. Although you should not have married following your decision at Tubunae, she was innocent, since she married you in innocence, without reservation. I wish that you could persuade her to live in continence as well so that you could give to God what you owe! If she does not agree to this, you must at least maintain your marital chastity and pray that God will lead you from your difficulties so that at some time you will be able to do what you cannot do now. You must continue now to love God and not the world. If you are called into military battle, hold fast to the faith and work for peace. Use the possessions of this world to do good, and do not fall into evil

as you seek or defend earthly goods. Your wife is not, or should not be, a hindrance in such matters.

I have written to you, my son, because of the affection I have for you. I love you because of God and not because of the world. I remember what is written, "Rebuke a wise man and he will love you; rebuke a fool and he will hate you even more" [Prov. 9:8]. I certainly regard you not as a fool but as a wise man.

XI.

Theodoret of Cyrrhus

THE CURE OF PAGAN DISEASES

Chapter 9. The Laws

My friends, I have put these thoughts together for you and hope that you will be attracted by them. If you do not find what you want to hear, you may laugh at them or make fun of them, or even refuse to listen to what they say. You must remember, however, that many times things that are very valuable come in rather cheap packages. For example, the precious pearl, an object of vanity for the rich, is found hidden in a lowly oyster that protects it and nourishes it. Those who spend a great deal of money to buy the pearl then throw the oyster away! The sparkling gems adorning the crown of a king came originally encased in stone that was completely worthless. The jewel cutters scraped away the stone and brought to light the beauty of the transparent and glittering jewel. The gold that people prize so highly is often found along with silver, copper, or iron and hidden in sand or earth. Workers must bore into the veins of gold or silver in the mines and retrieve the valuable ore bit by bit. Once the gold has been refined and hammered it is imprinted with the effigy of the emperor, and then it is no longer placed in a box made of gold but is rather placed in containers made of leather or wood, where it will be safer.

It is therefore quite understandable that the truths about God and humanity should be announced not in brilliant and majestic discourses but in quite simple and down-to-earth terms understood by everyone. It is quite appropriate that this great and wonderful treasure be contained in such a simple package.

Indeed, the force and power of these writings come from the comparison of the teachings of the legislators of Greece and

Rome with the teachings of our fishermen and tax collectors. By means of this comparison we can see how the former were unable to persuade their own neighbors to adopt their laws but the latter, the Galileans, were able to influence not only the Greeks and Romans but also the barbarians. All races have been willing to embrace the legislation of the gospel!

Minos [king of Crete], who according to the legend prided himself on having Zeus as his father, took the occasion of a visit to the temple of the gods to draw up a code of laws and to become the chief legislator of Crete. He was not, however, able to persuade the Sicilians, the Carthaginians, or even the Greeks to adopt his legal code. He was only able to force his own island to accept the laws, and even that did not last, because the Romans then came and conquered the world, so the Cretans too had to adopt the Roman laws.

It is said that Charondas was the first legislator of Italy and Sicily, but he was never able to get his neighbors, the Tyrrhenians, the Celts, the Iberians, or the Celtiberians, to adopt his laws. Why should he talk about neighboring countries, when we see that those residing there who praised these laws were not willing to continue to use them? They succumbed to the yoke of Roman law in the end.

Zaleucus gave the Locrians laws that, we are told by the historians, came from Athena. But neither the Acarnanians nor the Phocidians, nor even the Locrians themselves, accepted his laws. These were his own people and his nearest neighbors!

As for Lycurgus, those who praised his laws said that he had gone to Delphi to consult with the Pythian of Apollo before he was inspired to write the laws of the Lacedaemonians. He returned with a message that the Pythian had given him:

> You have come to my splendid sanctuary, O Lycurgus,
> You are dear to Zeus and to all who dwell in Olympus!
> I hesitate to say whether you are human or a god;
> I am inclined to look upon you as a god, O Lycurgus.
> You have come to seek good laws and, therefore,
>   you shall receive them.

Thus spoke the oracle concerning Lycurgus. Well, neither his great reputation, nor the splendor of Sparta, nor the oracle of Apollo Pythian could persuade the inhabitants of Argos, Tegea,

Mantinea, or Corinth, even though they lived close by, to adopt these Laconian constitutions. That is not to mention the many others! The Phliasians lived just one town away, and they were tied to the Spartans through an alliance that caused them to vote with the Spartans and remain under their control, but they never adopted the Spartan laws. I do not want to go on at great length about other legislators such as Apis of Argos, Mnaseas of Phoenicia, Demonax of Cyprus, Pagondas of Achaea, Archias of Cnidos, Eudoxus of Miletus, Philolaus of Thebes, Pittacus of Mytilene, and finally, Nestor of Pylos, whose words were described by Homer as being as "sweet as honey." I will not talk about legislators of other nations such as the famous Solon, Draco, or Cleisthenes, who were legislators of Athens. But the Athenians did not continue to follow the laws of Solon, or Draco, or Cleisthenes, nor did their closest neighbors, the Megarians, the Euboeans, or the Thebans. After the Athenians rejected these laws, just as the Locrians, the Thebans, and the other Greeks had done, they all came under the laws of Rome.

The Romans, on the other hand, assembled all the laws of the Greeks, the barbarians, and all the legislators whom they respected, and chose those laws which they considered best. They then forced all their subjects to abide by these laws. Even they, however, were not able to use either persuasion or violence to bring all people to adopt their Roman law. There were even some Roman subjects who had been freed from slavery but who refused to accept the laws of their benefactors. It turned out that neither the Ethiopians (whose country bordered the Egyptian Thebans), nor the innumerable tribes of the Ishmaelites, nor the Lazicans, Sanni, Abasgi, or other barbarians were willing to submit to the Roman laws.

On the other hand, our fishermen, our tax collectors, and our tentmaker have given to the world the laws of the gospel. It is not only among the Romans and their subjects but also among the Scythians, the Sarmatae, the Indians, the Ethiopians, the Persians, the Seres, the Hyrcanians, the Bactrians, the Britons, the Cimbre, the Germans, and indeed, all the nations of the world, that the laws of the Crucified have been accepted. This came about not through weapons and great armies, or force and cruelty, or the tactics of the Persians, but through persuasion and by showing the superiority of these laws. These laws were not

121

taught without risks to those who disseminated them. In many towns the disseminators were tortured, imprisoned, beaten, and injured, but they allowed this to happen. Those who were benefactors, saviors, and healers were at the same time treated as rebels and enemies who were hunted down, stoned, tied up, and imprisoned. Some of them were driven off with clubs, and others were placed in containers of water or fed to wild animals. Even when they were pierced with spears, the power of their laws was not broken, and indeed, they seemed to become much more powerful even after they were put to death.

It was subsequent to the death of such heroes that their teachings penetrated among the Persians, the Scythians, and even among many of the barbarians. In spite of the united efforts of the Romans and barbarians the power of these teachings continued. The Romans tried in many ways to destroy the memory of our fishermen and of our tentmaker but they only helped them to become even more famous and glorious. They superseded the laws of the Lycurgians, of Solon, Zaleucus, Charondas, Minos, and other lawmakers, but no one who accepted their new law protested. Their word became law. The memory of famous legislators had been extinguished while the Romans ruled cities of Greece. In Athens all had disappeared: the Areopagus, the Heliaea, the nearby tribunal of Delphi, the Council of the Five Hundred, the Eleven, the Thesmothetai, the Polemarchus, and a yearly gathering whose name was not well known except by those who wanted to read history books written by ancient authors.

The Lacedaemonians and the foreigners driven from Sparta could not be seen anymore; nor the enslaving of the islanders and naturalization of new citizens. Also gone was the impunity of the Lycurgian law toward the pederast and the loss of the meaning of marriage bonds. It must be remembered that the laws of Lycurgus, the "best of all lawmakers" according to the sages of the Greeks, were his own invention, according to the historians of Lacedaemonian politics. They permitted men and women who were already united by marriage to have relationships with other men and women, even the husbands and wives of others, and to produce children without regard to their marriage relationships. These were the kind of laws that attracted the admiration of Plato, and he formulated a plan for governing a city based upon them. But we must leave this philosophy of Plato until later, when we shall see that he believed himself to be the greatest of all lawmakers. For the moment we will look at the weakness of the Pythian laws and treat them alongside the Lycurgian code. It is known that as soon as Rome decided to abolish these laws in favor of her own, the Lycurgian code lost all of its uncontested force.

On the contrary, the laws of the fishermen, of our tax collectors, of our tentmaker could not be destroyed by Caius or Claudius, nor by Nero, their successor, who put to death the best of our legislators. He killed Peter and Paul but he could not destroy their laws. Neither could Vespasian, Titus, or Domitian! The last of these used all sorts of force against them; a great many people were tortured and put to death for following their laws. Trajan and Hadrian then waged a violent war against these laws, but even Trajan, who had destroyed the Persian Empire, who brought the Armenians under Roman control, and who subjugated the Scythians, was not able to destroy the laws of our fishermen and our tentmaker. Hadrian completely destroyed the towns of those who had crucified Jesus, but he failed in his attempt to force Jesus' followers into rejecting him. Antonius, his successor, and his son, Verus, brought back many trophies from their wars with the barbarians, and they forced the Roman yoke upon many people who had been free and independent, but they did not succeed, either through force or through persuasion, to make our people abandon their Savior whom they loved, for they carried the yoke of the cross with love. Many people were threatened, and many tortures were reinstituted under Commodus, Maximian, and many others down to the reign of Aurelius, Carus, and Carinus. There was the antireligious fury of Diocletian, Maximian, Maximinus, Maxentius, and Licinius, but the victory was won, not merely one by one, two by two, or three by three, but by the multitude of people who were killed because of their belief in Christ. It was by the dozens of thousands that they were killed. There were towns where churches that were filled with men, women, and children were burned, and it was on the very day that they had gathered to celebrate the passion and resurrection of our Lord that this event happened to churches throughout the Empire. But only a collection of stones was destroyed and not the collection of souls! The people of old knew all the harm that was directed against Christendom by Julian [the Apostate], and they have given us accounts of what they endured. Their oppressors were great in number and were supported by a great empire; they had defeated courageous barbarian armies; they had been brilliant in waging war; but their thousand methods did not succeed in overcoming those faithful, ill-trained, poor men who had their simple work to do and those women who worked each day with their hands. What shall I say about these men and women? Even their children, who did not understand the first thing about their God and Savior, were dragged away by those filled with hatred. But their treachery and cunning did not succeed in destroying the laws of our fishermen. The faithful became stronger in their faith, for the oppression was like throwing oil on a fire. Instead of putting the fire out, they merely affirmed the truths about the Christian faith. It is like the story of the burning bush that was not destroyed by the fire. In the same way the persecuted people were not destroyed by the fire of their persecutors. On the contrary, with trees that are cut down, the roots grow deeper and produce more shoots than were there in the first place. One sees that the same thing happened when the faithful were suppressed for their numbers increased as others came and were taught the gospel. The blood of the Christians became a river of nourishment for those who entered the faith.

We can see with our own eyes that the number of believers is greater now than it was in the past. Even the children of our persecutors have come to reject the violence of their parents and have entered the community of the persecuted. Hellenism has disappeared and fallen into oblivion, but the doctrine of our fishermen has blossomed and grown so that their God is proclaimed as the God of the universe. In the towns we find many people who believe this; the same is true in the countryside. The mountains have been freed from the fear of the pagan shrines of past ages, and the choirs of the ascetics are now there singing the praises of the Crucified and of his Father and the Holy Spirit!

If one imagines that it was the piety of the emperors that gave strength to the doctrines of the fishermen, this only proves the truth of the doctrine. Indeed, emperors would not have rejected the old laws, the traditions and customs of the past, and their ancestral heritage, if they had not been drawn to accept the truths of the one while rejecting the fables of the others.

Why should you not be reminded of the wars that were waged in the past against the church? It would be difficult to disregard such things. If so many powerful emperors have tried with all their might to destroy a religion but have failed even to shake its walls, one would have to be idiotic or completely stupid not to believe that the power of the fishermen is divine but to believe that these things happened because of the power of the emperors.

In order to make my point more clearly, consider what the Persians have done in our own day. What suffering have they failed to inflict upon the faithful? They have suffocated them, mutilated their hands and feet, cut off their ears and noses, made them carry heavy shackles to inflict suffering, and chained them before throwing them into great ditches filled with rats that devoured them. Yes, with such tortures, and many more, they were able to mutilate the body and inflict death, but they could not rob believers of the treasures of their faith. They could force many people to come under their laws, but they could not force the believers to deny the laws of their fishermen.

The Persians, who at one time followed the laws of Zoroaster, had without scruple indulged in sexual relations with their mothers, sisters, and even daughters, because they believed that these immoral practices were allowed by their law. When the laws of the fishermen were preached to them, they threw the laws of Zoroaster at his feet, because they recognized them to be immoral, and they embraced evangelical chastity. They also had learned from Zoroaster to feed corpses to dogs and birds of prey, but today all those who have been converted to the faith have given up this practice and now, without fear, bury the laws that had defended this custom. They do not even tremble as they stand before their cruel executioners, for they have an even greater fear of the tribunal of Christ. They fear not the mocking of others but only that they might lose their senses in that moment of suffering. In the midst of such laws they have received the men from Galilee! They have not feared the Roman Empire, for they have joined the empire of the Crucified! Augustus and Trajan, who had defeated the Persian Empire, could not enforce Roman law among them. But then as a gift from heaven came the writings of Peter, Paul, John, Matthew, Luke, and Mark, and the teachings of these strangers and newcomers were accepted.

The Massagetae at one time believed that anyone who died from a cause other than being slaughtered was most unfortunate. They also had laws commanding that old men be sacrificed and eaten. When they heard the laws of the fishermen and the tent-maker, they were horrified at their detestable banquets and murders.

The Tibarenians, who had the custom of throwing old people off rocky cliffs, abolished this abominable law when they heard the laws of the gospel. The Hyrcanians and the Caspians no longer fed dead bodies to the dogs and the Scythians no longer buried the living along with the dead who had loved them. In such transformations you see the great power of the laws of the fishermen!

These laws have united the barbarians who govern themselves, whereas Plato, the greatest of the philosophers, was not able to have his laws accepted even by his own countrymen, the Athenians. This was a correct response on their part! His laws are absolutely ridiculous! Do not get the idea that I merely am trying to slander the philosopher. Listen, instead, to the laws that he devised.

He decided that the women, not only young girls but also the older ones, should do gymnastics naked. When he saw that his critics began to laugh, he said,

> As for the man who laughs at the sight of naked women, who exercise for excellent reasons, he is pulling from his own wisdom the unripe fruit of laughter, and indicates that he has no understanding about what he laughs at or what he does. [*Republic* V.457]

Elsewhere he wrote,

> In regard to girls I will use the same language that I do about boys. I insist that the girls do exactly the same exercises. In explaining my doctrine I have no reservations that horsemanship and gymnastics are both appropriate for women and men alike. [*Laws* VII.804]

Is it not laughable when you hear such theories? It is a fact of nature that each sex has special functions: the women spin wool, and the men cultivate the soil and wage war. Homer also made such a distinction; for example, in his verses he has Hector say to Andromache,

> Let us go back to our home now. You shall attend to your own work: the spinning wheel and the loom, and to see that the servants do their work. War is men's business, and to take part in this war is the task of every man. . . . [*Iliad* VI.490–92]

The philosopher did not even make the distinction which the poet made. Instead, he commanded the women to do gymnastics completely naked and to ride the horse. Of course, such ideas bring their own results. This is what he then says:

> As for the question to know whether the people of whom I have just spoken are of a suitable age for marriage, that is to be decided by a judge who will inspect the males completely naked and the women naked up to their navel. [*Laws* XI.925]

That man who made these laws has obviously forgotten what the wife of Candaul said when her husband asked her to show her naked body:

> The woman who takes off her clothes is taking away her chastity at the same time.

Here you see the philosopher who takes away the chastity of married women and who teaches them immodesty! He wrote the same thing in the *Laws:*

> Finally, it is for an important reason that the activities of boys and girls be organized before they are paired together. They should be taught to dance so that they may learn to look at and be looked at. With consideration given to good reason and their age they are to be undressed within the limits of modesty. [*Laws* VI.771–72]

From my point of view I see faults in what he proposes and I do not see any good to come from it. Undoubtedly, it will lead women to become immodest and not to mind being seen naked or to see naked men. This will lead to occasions of sexual indulgence. It is quite evident that the sight of naked bodies will lead the men and women to disordered love affairs.

In order to convince you I do not want to dwell on the damage caused by these laws, lest you think that I am merely slandering

Plato and not arguing by refuting his ideas. Let us look at his magnificent laws concerning marriage and I will make some just criticism of them. In the *Republic* he says,

> Wives will be in common among all our men. No woman will live with any one man privately. The children also will be in common and the father will not know his son nor the son his father. [*Republic* V.457]

He also adds,

> There will be a lawgiver who will choose men and women to be paired as best he can according to their natures. Both sexes will live together and share the same house and meals. None of them will possess anything in particular. They will come together in the gymnasium as well as in the rest of their daily lives. I believe that they will be led by natural instinct to pair up. Does this not seem to be inevitable? It is by no means a geometric necessity but a drive which springs from love and which is stronger than the former in directing and controlling the masses. [*Republic* V.458].

It is not necessary that I go on at great length in order to show that the philosopher has endorsed a communal life with women and that he imagines the necessity for a communal sex life. As they live together, he said, let them share their meals, let them exercise together, and let them allow their natural desires to guide them into uniting with others. He also says that children are a common good and therefore they should have no scruples about having children by the first person to come along. The children belong to all when they are born. After thinking this over, Socrates asked, "Do you not think it an imposition to have someone select pairs rather than allowing it to happen naturally?" Plato responded, "It certainly is not a matter of mathematical necessity but a necessity of love, which is much stronger and which can be used to control the masses."

From my point of view I am amazed at the impudence of people today who try to interpret Plato or to manipulate what he has said. They try to cover up the fact that Plato advocated a free-sex community, by claiming that he wanted merely a community of friends. They are not listening to what he said: "Have in common the living quarters, the dining room, the gymnasium, and allow natural drives to determine with whom you have sexual relations." Perhaps they do this because they are embarrassed by the ridiculous laws of the philosopher and they want to undo the error of their master. We must always remember his own words: "We should honor a friend; we should honor truth. Yet, even though both of these are to be honored, we must honor truth as the higher" [*Republic* X.595].

We also need to look at some other ideas in the philosopher's laws. He says, "A woman will give birth to children for the state for twenty years beginning with her twentieth year; a man will procreate for the state from the time that he reaches his prime physical condition until he is fifty-five years old" [*Republic* V.460]. This may not look as if it is dangerous, but it does have serious consequences for marriage, and one should not laugh about it but should cry over such laws and condemn these infamous laws to the fire! Plato says, in effect, "When men and women have passed the age for procreation, they may freely unite with others, but they must ensure that any child conceived will not see the light of day. If they should allow such a child to be born, it must not be given any food nor be given to someone else to raise." What kind of Eschetus [King Eschetus the Ogre] or Phalaris could have thought up such laws? Who ever went to such limits in devising laws that justified such murders? It is recommended that a fetus not be allowed to develop and be born but that it be destroyed with abortive drugs. In any case, even if the child is born, it faces death from hunger, or the cold, or even from wild animals. What kind of extreme cruelty has ever surpassed this one!

There you see the laws that Plato devised regarding marriage and procreation. What other forms of sexual immorality did he teach? It is easy to discover if one wants to know! Indeed, he says that those who engage in unnatural sexual relations will be happy on earth and even blessed in heaven. "It is not of small value," he says in effect, "as the price to pay for such [passionate] love. For they are no longer relegated by law to a life in the shadows and an underground journey. Now the law will protect those who lead such a life and they will begin a journey heavenward. They will lead radiant lives and travel together in blessedness taking flight with their relationship of love" [*Phaedrus* 256]. After this he concludes, "O Youth! See what heavenly rewards your lover will give to you!" He makes such observations not in regard to chaste lovers but about those whose love is disordered. All of this is quite clear in his dialogues. Such laws were not even thought up by Nero, the most abysmal Roman emperor, or by the Assyrian Sardanapale, famous for his love of pleasure and the good life. For my part, I believe that those who are so completely caught up in such passions lose any feeling of pleasure and merely become slaves to their way of life.

Now we must speak about the abnormal laws that Plato instituted in regard to murder. He orders that one who kills one's own servant is not to be punished. He condemns to a simple fine one who kills the servant of someone else in anger. If someone kills a free person in anger, the killer receives two years' exile; if the killing was premeditated, three years' exile. Should the killer return and kill again, that person receives perpetual exile. He legislates in the same fashion against fathers who kill their children, against children who kill their fathers, husbands who kill their wives, and wives who kill their husbands!

Now you see! The philosopher gathered together these laws but never was able to point to one person who lived by them; not a citizen, a stranger, a city dweller, a country dweller, a Greek, a barbarian, a slave, a free person, an ordinary man or an ordinary woman, a young person or an old person, an educated person or an illiterate.

For my part, I wish only to explain to you the laws of the fishermen, the tax collectors, and the tentmaker which have been given for all people. I believe that after you compare the one set of laws with the other you will admire the divine radiance of our laws.

The philosopher, we have said, admired unrestrained homosexuality, and he indicated that its reward would be three times holy! Our Savior, on the other hand, has rebuked not only the evil deed itself but everything related to it. "Whoever," he said, "looks at a woman with lust has already committed adultery with her in his heart" [Matt. 5:28]. Without scruple the philosopher made a law that people should unite freely among themselves. The Author of nature, who created human nature, decreed that one man and one woman should be united and that marriage was not to be dissolved except for one unique occasion, namely, the one that truly tears apart the marriage bond. "Whoever," he says, "divorces his wife except for unfaithfulness will make of her an adulteress; and whoever marries such a person will commit adultery" [Matt 5·32].

Because of this he commands that one should support one's spouse even if she should talk too much or be addicted to drink, or even if she should become aggressive! But if she violates the laws of marriage and goes with another man, then he orders the breaking of the marriage bond. He also made similar regulations through the mouth of the tentmaker, who said in his Letter to the Corinthians, "It is good not to touch a woman in order to avoid any temptation. Each man should have a wife and each woman a husband" [1 Cor. 7:1–2]. Can you see the difference between the laws of the philosopher and of the tentmaker? The tentmaker prescribes that every woman should have her own husband and every man his own wife. The former, however, prescribes that all women should be in common to all men.

The tentmaker also gives laws related to continence. He does not allow the woman to abstain from sexual intercourse if the husband does not consent, nor may the husband abstain if the wife does not consent. "The woman," he says, "does not rule over her own body, but the husband does. In the same way, the husband does not rule over his body, but the wife does. Do not refuse each other unless both are agreed" [1 Cor. 7:4–5]. If one observes chastity but at the wrong time, one will become frustrated in doing what one feels is right. Then, becoming insensitive to that which is true perfection, one must, as Saint Paul says, "turn to fasting and prayer that you may then come together again" [1 Cor. 7:5]. Thus, according to the laws of nature, he says that "out of fear that Satan should tempt you" we must beware lest Satan take over within us. This, he says, "comes about because of your incontinence." For the celibate such laws do not apply, for that person must take into account other matters. "That person who is not married," he says, should be devoted to the things of our Lord and how to please the Lord. Those who are married have concerns about worldly things and must try to please their spouses [1 Cor. 7:32–33]. He also applies the same understanding to women, teaching them to observe virginity so that they may be free of worries.

My friends, admire what Paul has taught, and adore him about whom he talks! Take another look at the laws about murder. While the philosopher does not demand punishment even for one who kills one's father, our Savior condemns and speaks harshly against any injustice. "Whoever," he says, "is overcome by anger against a brother will face the tribunal; and if he says to his brother, 'Raca!' he is liable for judgment by the Sanhedrin, and if he says, 'You fool!' he is liable to the fire of hell" [Matt. 5:22]. He even threatens punishment for engaging in useless talk, and he demands that we do good not only to our friends but also to our enemies. "Love your enemies," he says, "and do good to those who persecute you" [Matt. 5:44]. Finally, he offers a reward that is far greater than what is deserved by those who fight for their faith: "You must be children of your Father in heaven, for he makes the sun to rise on the evil as well as on the good, and he will send a shower of rain on the righteous as well as on the wicked" [Matt. 5:45]. He also gave us laws that prohibit our making long speeches for our defense. It suffices to say either yes or no in order to underline what we are saying [Matt. 5:33–37]. He also says that those who are poor have a more perfect life: "Whoever does not renounce everything that he possesses cannot become my disciple" [Luke 14:33]. By thus instituting such a strict code of life, he does not promise any kind of satisfaction in this life but promises only poverty, misery, injury, beatings, and injuries from all sides: "In the world you will have tribulation" [John 16:33], and, "Blessed are you when you are insulted and persecuted and have evil things said about you falsely for my sake. Rejoice and be glad, for your reward will be great in heaven" [Matt. 5:11–12]. He has emphasized the pains and the dangers, but he also promises rewards and crowns at the end of this life. In another passage he says, "If they persecute me, they will also persecute you; if they keep my word, they will also keep yours" [John 15:20]. And elsewhere, "If they have even called the master of the house Beelzebul, how much more will they persecute those who live in that household!" [Matt. 10:25].

Now that you have seen what our laws are, it is truly right that we should admire those who taught them and those who believe in them. Indeed, they received them from him, and without promise of riches or power or physical strength in this life they went out with faith in the promises of what is to come. They accepted their sufferings and were supported in all danger as they traveled across the world teaching every nation. We must not praise those who received the laws less than their teachers. They often did not find anything brilliant or outstanding in their preachers, but they did find the words of the fishermen and the tentmaker. Often they faced extreme poverty, and although they did not have the next day's nourishment that they needed, they were not deterred, for they knew that they should not be concerned for the morrow. They believed what they had been taught, and they rejected the laws of the society in which they lived. They abandoned the traditions of their ancestors, and like their teachers, devoted their lives to passing on what they had learned. They too were outcasts and forced to pass through the mud and the storms. They have, in the same way, veneration for those who were exposed to many dangers right up to their death. They are seen as heroes because of the treasure that fills their tombs and that is supplied to all in abundance.

Now, my friends, let us reflect on the power of their laws. The Romans, the Persians, and those who lived outside the Empire all gave up their own laws when they saw the weaknesses in them. The laws of Lycurgus and Solon were destroyed not by outward forces but from what was within. Neither Apollo Pythian nor Athena Polias was concerned with preserving their laws, and the laws were abolished when the Romans decided to replace them with their own. Could one of you, my friends, show me a Spartan who is ready to die for the laws of Lycurgus, or an Athenian for those of Solon, or a Locrian for those of Zaleucus, or a Cretan for those of Minos? None of you can do that! We, on the contrary, can point to dozens of thousands who were ready to give their lives for the laws of the fishermen and the tentmaker. As a witness we have the tombs of the martyrs, which are the pride of the towns, the ornaments of the fields, the source of blessing for strangers as well as the people of the region.

Since the differences can clearly be seen as they exist among the laws of various lawmakers, it makes their laws appear as human inventions, whereas our laws appear as health-giving, divine gifts. Receive them, my friends, as God-given gifts and do not reject the One who has given them to you with great kindness and generosity. You too will come to know their perfect divine nature if you will leave aside your prejudices and accept them willingly.

Bibliography

PRIMARY SOURCES

Ambrose. *De officiis ministrorum,* ed. J. G. Krabinger. Tübingen, 1857.

Aristides. In C. Vona, *L'Apologia di Aristide: Introduzione, Versione dal Siriaco e Commento,* 71–114. Lateranum n.s. 16/1–4. Rome, 1950.

———.*Apologia Aristidis.* In *Texts and Studies* 1/1, ed. J. A. Robinson, 100–112. Cambridge, 1891.

Augustine. *Epistulae CLXXXIX et CCXX.* In *Corpus Scriptorum Ecclesiasticorum Latinorum* 57:131–37, 431–41. Vienna, 1911.

Basil. In Y. Courtonne, *Saint Basile, Lettres: Text établi et traduit* 1:52–57. Paris, 1957.

Clement of Alexandria. *Quis dives salvetur?* In *Die griechischen Christlichen Schriftsteller,* vol. 17, ed. O. Stählin, 157–91. Leipzig, 1909.

Cyprian. *De opere et eleemosynis.* In *Corpus Scriptorum Ecclesiasticorum Latinorum* 3/1:371–94. Vienna, 1868.

Didache. In J. P. Audet, *La Didachè. Etudes bibliques.* Paris, 1958.

Elvira, Council of. In C. J. Hefele, *A History of the Christian Councils,* trans. W. R. Clark, 138–72. Edinburgh, 1871.

Tertullian. *Apologeticum.* In *Corpus Christianorum,* series Latina, 1:77–171. Turnholt, 1954.

———.*De Idololatria.* In *Corpus Christianorum,* series Latina, 2:1101–24. Turnholt, 1954.

Theodoret of Cyrrhus. In R. P. Canivet, *Théodore de Cyr: Thérapeutique des maladies helléniques,* 336–59. Sources chrétiennes 57. Paris, 1958.

SECONDARY WORKS

Cunningham, A. *The Early Church and the State.* Philadelphia: Fortress Press, 1982.

Forell, G. W. *History of Christian Ethics,* vol. 1. Minneapolis: Augsburg Pub. House, 1979.

Frend, W. H. C. *The Rise of Christianity.* Philadelphia: Fortress Press, 1984.

Grant, R. M. *Augustus to Constantine.* New York: Harper & Row, 1970.

————.*Early Christianity and Society.* New York: Harper & Row, 1977.

Greenslade, S. L. *Schism in the Early Church.* London: SCM Press, 1964.

Harnack, A. *Militia Christi: The Christian Religion and the Military in the First Three Centuries.* Philadelphia: Fortress Press, 1981.

Hengel, M. *Property and Riches in the Early Church.* Philadelphia: Fortress Press, 1974.

Laeuchli, S. *Power and Sexuality: The Emergence of Canon Law at the Synod of Elvira.* Philadelphia: Temple Univ. Press, 1972.

Macquarrie, J., ed. *A Dictionary of Ethics.* London: SCM Press, 1967.

Troeltsch, E. *The Social Teaching of the Christian Churches,* vol. 1. Chicago: Univ. of Chicago Press, 1981.